The World of
Rubens

TIME-LIFE LIBRARY OF ART

The World of
Rubens

1577 - 1640

by C. V. Wedgwood
and
the Editors of TIME-LIFE BOOKS

TIME-LIFE INTERNATIONAL (NEDERLAND) B.V.

About the Author

C. V. Wedgwood, one of England's leading historians, specializes in European history of the 17th Century. Her books include *The Thirty Years War, William the Silent* and three historical narratives on the English Civil War and its aftermath: *The King's Peace, The King's War* and *A Coffin for King Charles*. Miss Wedgwood is a member of the Institute for Advanced Study at Princeton, New Jersey, and was guest lecturer at Bryn Mawr College for the year 1963-1964. In recognition of her scholarship, she was named Commander, Order of the British Empire, in 1956. She holds honorary degrees from Glasgow University and from Harvard.

The Consulting Editor

H. W. Janson is Professor of Fine Arts at New York University. Among his numerous books and publications are his definitive *History of Art, The Sculpture of Donatello* and *The Story of Painting for Young People*, which he co-authored with his wife.

The Consultants for This Book

Michael Jaffé is First University Lecturer in art history at Cambridge, England. He is the author of numerous articles on Italian and Flemish art of the 16th and 17th Centuries, particularly on Rubens, and is the editor of the two-volume book *Van Dyck's Antwerp Sketchbook*.

Jane Costello, Professor of Fine Arts at New York University, is the co-author with Walter Friedlander of *The Drawings of Nicolas Poussin*. She has taught two series of art courses on television, one of which was "The Age of Rubens."

On the Cover

A Child's Head, painted about 1618, is thought by art historians to be Rubens' portrait of his first child, Clara Serena, who died in 1623 at the age of 12. The complete picture, of which this is a detail, appears on page 18.

End Papers

Rubens made these two drawings as models for a woodcut. When joined they compose a variation on his delightful painting *The Garden of Love (page 188)*. The Metropolitan Museum of Art, Fletcher Fund, 1958.

ISBN 900658 57 6

Contents

I

An Abundance of Gifts

A master at painting flamboyant pictures filled with action, Rubens was nevertheless able to look at himself candidly, as this self-portrait suggests. Made within the last decade of his life, the sketch is a study for the painting that appears on page 184.

Self-Portrait, c. 1635

Peter Paul Rubens was that rarity, a great creative genius who also possessed every physical and psychological attribute necessary for private happiness and public success: good health, good looks, good intellect, abundant energy, a well-balanced temperament and, added to all this, a clear head for business.

He was a happy man. His pictures leave no doubt of that. He delighted in the visible world—in its color, texture, form and movement. Most of all he delighted in the plastic and supple beauty of the human body. Although he took pleasure in material things, he was also deeply imbued with the intense and exalted religious faith of his time. But whether he painted a blonde Venus with attendant nymphs or a grave Virgin with her Child in her arms, a radiant allegory of cloud-borne figures or the solid, fertile landscape near his home, his work was a hymn of praise for the beauty of the world.

Rubens lived from 1577 to 1640, during that period which historians call the Counter Reformation because it was dominated by the revival of the Roman Catholic Church and its attempt to combat the effects of the Protestant Reformation. It was a time of conflict, remarkable for great achievements of the human spirit and intellect, but also for greed, intolerance and cruelty. During Rubens' lifetime, scientists like Galileo, Johannes Kepler and William Harvey reshaped man's vision of his own world and the universe; the mathematician and philosopher René Descartes sounded a call to reason that profoundly affected man's thinking; Catholic saints such as Francis de Sales and Teresa of Avila dedicated their lives to revitalizing the spiritual strength of the Church.

But the reverse side of the age was correspondingly dark. Witch-hunting, the frightful spawn of religious zeal mixed with blind superstition, made the 16th and 17th Centuries a nightmare of horror and death at the stake for thousands of men and women throughout Europe who had supposedly committed crimes against man and nature. The Inquisition, revived from medieval times to seek out enemies of the Church of Rome, inevitably led to the persecution and torture of suspected heretics. Religious wars repeatedly disturbed the peace of Europe; the most destructive of them, the Thirty Years' War, harrowed Germany during the years of Rubens' greatest success. Rubens' own country, the Netherlands, was torn apart during his lifetime by a struggle for independence from Spain which began 10 years before he was born and did not end until eight years after his death. It comes as a shock to realize that Rubens painted his luminous pictures at a time of so much darkness, violence and distress.

Was Rubens then insensitive to the realities of his time or indifferent to suffering? On the contrary, he was a keen observer of the political scene and an active participant. His advice was valued by the rulers of the Netherlands and he was several times entrusted with delicate diplomatic missions. His letters bear witness to his concern for the state of Europe and the sufferings caused by unceasing war.

Yet Rubens' temperament led him to dwell more frequently on the blessings of humanity than on its misfortunes. Few great painters have more confidently and consistently expressed the bounty of nature and the potential happiness of man. It may be that he owed something of the immense popularity of his art during his life to the need that men feel for reassurance in time of stress—for a vision of the world that reminds them that their Creator, after He had completed His work, had looked upon it and found it good.

Another reason for Rubens' popularity was that his art so perfectly expressed the intellectual spirit of the day. In his lifetime the culture of Western Europe was both Christian and Classical; the Classical revival of the Renaissance and the religious revival of the Reformation and Counter Reformation that followed it had come together into a single intellectual stream. Catholic and Protestant scholars alike devoted themselves to the study of Greek and Roman antiquity, but they were equally concerned to extend Christian knowledge and establish Christian doctrine. It was becoming possible to reconcile the material beauty of the Classical heritage with the spiritual teaching of the Christian Churches.

In Rome at the turn of the 17th Century this dynamic union of Classicism and Christian zeal was beginning to make itself felt in the world of art in a new expression that was soon to flower as the Baroque style. The new spirit invigorated painting, sculpture and architecture with fresh energy, shaped them with dramatic effects of light, color and movement, and infused them with a strong appeal to the emotions of the spectator.

Rubens found this ardent expression entirely congenial to his own convictions. He blended an enthusiasm for antiquity and his deep personal piety into a powerful pictorial art, taking inspiration from pagan sources to give a new dimension to Christian themes, and treating mythological subjects with a warm humanity. By this imaginative fusion of Christian and Classical images he delighted and inspired his contemporaries as no other painter did.

Not only was Rubens' art an inspiration to his own and succeeding generations but it also served as an organic link between Italy and the North. Before Rubens, Italian and Flemish art had typically pursued separate courses. Flemish painting was highly realistic, oriented toward landscape and portraiture, distinguished by graphic detail and conserva-

This 17th Century drawing of Antwerp's crowded harbor, the work of an anonymous artist of the Flemish school, shows how the city prospered in the days before Rubens was born. As many as 100 ships at a time lay in the wide river port unloading cargoes of French wine, Baltic grain, Italian silks, Venetian glass and Asian spices. More than 1,000 commercial firms in Antwerp exported beer, tapestries, linen, pottery, and beautiful gold and silver wares.

THE BRITISH MUSEUM, LONDON

tive composition. On the other hand, the Renaissance had endowed Italian art with great imaginative freedom, monumental proportions and grandiose themes. Though trained in the North, Rubens achieved maturity as an artist during the years he spent in Italy, and he successfully assimilated the two traditions as no other artist had done before him. He gave new direction to the visual arts of the North by his own exuberant and individual interpretation of the powerful artistic currents of Rome. Thus Rubens was a figure of critical significance in the development of Western art, as well as a great painter in his own right.

Rubens was born on June 28, 1577, at Siegen in the German province of Westphalia, the sixth child of Jan and Maria Rubens. Nine years earlier, Jan and Maria had fled their native city of Antwerp to escape religious persecution. Jan, though originally a Roman Catholic, had developed a sympathy for the Protestant doctrines of John Calvin and this was dangerous heresy in a land controlled by the Catholic King of Spain.

The Rubens family settled first in Cologne, where Jan, a lawyer of some distinction, became secretary to the Princess of Orange, wife of the active leader of resistance to Spain. The Princess, a passionate and unbalanced woman, took Jan for her lover while the Prince was away. The intrigue was discovered and the guilty pair arrested. The Princess was divorced and died insane some years later. Jan was imprisoned, and fully expected to pay for his folly with his life. But Maria worked unceasingly for his release, raising money for bail and even making her way into the Prince's presence once or twice to plead her husband's cause personally.

The letters she wrote Jan in prison indicate the depth of her devotion. She begs him to be of good courage and assures him that she has forgiven him: "How could I be so hard as to burden you who are in such great distress; where there has been such a long friendship as ours, how could there now be so much hatred as to make me unable to forgive a little fault against me. . . . I pray to God for you; our children do the same, and send many greetings and are very anxious to see you, as I am. . . . Please do not say again 'unworthy husband,' for it is all forgiven."

After two years, Maria succeeded in her quest, and in 1573 Jan was released on bail and permitted to live with his family in the little town of Siegen. In 1578, a year after the birth of Peter Paul, Jan was allowed to return to Cologne, and finally, in 1583, he was given a full pardon.

In spite of the anxieties of exile and the misfortunes of his father, the home in which Peter Paul grew up seems to have been calm and harmonious. In later years he would remember Cologne as the scene of a happy childhood. He inherited the best qualities of both his parents. Like his mother he had a generous and steady temperament and a capacity for loyalty and affection, and he also probably absorbed her methodical ways with time and money. From his father came a quick intelligence and easy charm. Jan Rubens himself undertook the education of the boy, and implanted in him a lasting love for learning and literature.

But when Peter Paul was not quite 10 years old, his father died, leaving Maria and her children to their own slender resources in a foreign land. The oldest son, Jan-Baptist, was already grown up and had gone to pursue his studies in Italy. Death, so common even among the young at a time of limited medical knowledge, had taken three children, and Maria was left with a daughter in her twenties and two boys, Philip, now about 13, and Peter Paul, three years younger.

Maria owned a little property back home in Antwerp and so she returned there with her children. She could safely do so, since she had reconciled her family with the Catholic Church. Indeed, it is possible that she had never altogether shared her husband's Protestant beliefs, though Peter Paul and Philip had both been baptized as Lutherans.

Although Peter Paul did not see Antwerp until he was 10, the Rubens family had lived there as respected citizens for at least two centuries. So, it was not a strange city, but a place full of kinsfolk and friends. Though born in exile, Rubens always felt himself to be a true son of Antwerp.

At the time Jan and Maria Rubens fled in 1568, Antwerp was the hub of commerce in Northern Europe. Situated on the River Scheldt, some 50 miles from its outlet on the North Sea, with a capacious and well-organized port, the city received the merchandise of all Germany overland, while its ships sailed north to Scandinavia and England, west across the Atlantic to America, south to Spain and Portugal and through the Mediterranean to Italy. Many colonies of foreign merchants lived in Antwerp—Spanish and Portuguese, Italian, German and English. It was not only the chief money market of Europe but one of the great cities of the world.

A resident Italian diplomat, Ludovico Guicciardini, wrote an account of Antwerp at the height of its prosperity. He praised the magnificent port and busy streets, the splendid cathedral with its harmonious carillon of 33 bells, the majestic town hall and the well-designed bourse, or exchange, where the bankers and merchants of many nations met. There were fine schools, numerous painters and a printing establishment, founded in 1555 by Christophe Plantin, that was one of the finest in Europe, remarkable for its elegant production and scholarly proofreading.

The people of Antwerp, Guicciardini wrote, "are humane, civilized, ingenious [and have] much worldly good sense; most of them, including many women, speak three or four languages. . . . Men and women alike, of all ages, dress extremely well. . . . At all hours you will find feasts, banquets and dances. . . . In a word, every neighborhood and every street bears witness to the wealth, power, pomp and splendor of the town."

That is what Antwerp had been like in its palmy days, when Maria Rubens was a girl. It was no longer so when she returned with her children in 1587. Antwerp had suffered more disastrously than any other town in the Netherlands, partly from Spanish rule, partly from the revolt against it. The events that caused this sad condition started long before Rubens was born, but they were very important in shaping the political and religious loyalties that dominated his life.

Spanish control in the Netherlands had been established in 1555. Before that the Netherlands—that part of Europe which we today call Holland, Belgium and Luxembourg—consisted of nearly a score of provinces, each with its separate government, bound into a political federation and united under a feudal ruler, the Duke of Burgundy. The last Duke of Burgundy had died in battle in 1477 leaving only one child, a daughter. She married the Archduke Maximilian of Austria, who became head of the Habsburg dynasty and Holy Roman Emperor. In due course their grandson inherited Spain, the Netherlands, the Austrian dominions, and in 1519 was elected Holy Roman Emperor as well. He is known to history as Charles V. He had been educated in the Netherlands, and while he ruled, the independence of the Netherlands was respected.

But in 1555 Charles V made an odd division of his vast inheritance. He assigned the Austrian dominions (and the title of Emperor) to his brother Ferdinand—but he gave the Netherlands to his son Philip II, King of Spain. Philip had been brought up in Spain, never liked nor understood the Netherlands, and as a deeply devout Roman Catholic was resolved to root out the heresies that had gained a hold there during the Reformation. An explosion of Protestant rioting in 1566 gave him the excuse to send in a Spanish governor and Spanish troops. The governor was the austere and ruthless Duke of Alva, who instituted a reign of terror. It was in the following year that Jan Rubens fled the country. He was wise to have done so. Hundreds of victims went to the gallows or the block under Alva's orders and many of them were prominent citizens of Antwerp, including the burgomaster himself.

Gradually, resistance stiffened, particularly in the North, where William of Orange, the most powerful of all Netherlandish nobles, took up the fight. Within a few years William had liberated the maritime provinces of Holland and Zeeland, and by 1579, six smaller provinces had joined them in a pact of independence.

The southern part of the Netherlands was less fortunate. In 1576 the Spanish army, demoralized by defeat in the North and by lack of pay, ran amok in Antwerp. The center of the city, including 1,400 houses and the town hall, was burned down, and more than 7,000 people were killed in the streets. In anger and despair the citizens rose against their oppressors and for a time joined with the North in the fight against Spain. But the Roman Catholic religion and the old dynastic loyalties had deeper roots in the South than in the North and the alliance broke down. Then in 1585 Antwerp, after a long siege, capitulated to the Spanish forces. For the next 130 years, the Southern Netherlands remained under the rule of Spain.

When Maria Rubens and her children went home in 1587, the situation in the Netherlands had stabilized on a basis of division between the independent United Provinces in the North, where Protestantism in the Calvinist form was a strong force, and the Spanish-controlled, largely Catholic South. There was almost continuous war on the frontier between them, intensified at intervals by French and English intervention. The Spaniards did not for many years give up their efforts to reconquer the rebellious Northern provinces, but other European powers soon recognized the independence of the new Dutch Republic. It was already very powerful at sea, and in fierce economic competition with the South. For its part, the South, at this time usually called the Spanish Netherlands, accepted the King of Spain as its legal ruler by right of descent from the Dukes of Burgundy. Its citizens' memories of a rich and glorious past were bound up with the old ducal dynasty, and a tactful gov-

In November 1576, during three days of uncontrolled rioting, Spanish troops brought Antwerp's commercial prosperity virtually to an end. Mutinous soldiers killed thousands, destroyed property and robbed rich and poor, Catholic and Calvinist, foreigner and Fleming. The contemporary engraving above shows street fighting, with the Town Hall ablaze in the background; below is a massacre on the banks of the River Scheldt.

Rubens often copied the work of other artists to provide himself with a source book of costumes of earlier periods for use in his own paintings. These two drawings are based on figures by a Flemish artist named Antoine de Succa, who presumably drew them for an illustrated history of the Netherlands. Rubens preserved all de Succa's details of dress, and made careful color notes.

ernment could turn this local pride into loyalty for a new regime. And gradually the governors appointed by Spain were becoming more tactful.

Rubens apparently never had any doubt as to where his loyalties lay. Throughout his life he remained a dutiful subject of the Catholic rulers of the Spanish Netherlands. One reason for his devotion is perhaps to be found in the favor that they showed to Antwerp.

No doubt when he was a boy he heard his mother describe the city's vanished glories. But to a child the past is a kind of fairy tale; it is not real. Rubens never saw these splendors with his own eyes. When he first came to Antwerp the city was still in deep distress. The population had sunk to 45,000—less than half what it had been 20 years earlier. The woeful damage of the sack in 1576 and traces of the long siege could be seen in battered, derelict buildings, churches with broken and boarded windows, deserted streets, burned-out suburbs. The seas were unsafe and the mouth of the Scheldt was blocked by the Dutch. The once-flourishing colonies of foreign merchants had dwindled; some had vanished altogether and taken their trade elsewhere. The surrounding country was a waste of abandoned farms and ruined villages. Famine had followed war and there can have been little music, feasting or fine clothes in Antwerp in the first years after the Rubens family's return.

Gradually a revival began. The Spanish government made Antwerp the center of the network of finance and provisioning that supported its armies in the Netherlands. This restored something of the city's importance as a European money market. The Dutch, in spite of the continuing frontier war, began to let ships pass up the Scheldt on payment of a toll. Overseas trade thus became possible again, though it was never to be what it had once been. The wasted countryside was slowly brought back under cultivation. Gradually, thanks to the stubborn industry of the people, a modified prosperity returned. The esthetic and intellectual life of the city revived. The Plantin printing press recovered from the setback of the lean years, and the studios of the Antwerp painters once more had commissions from churches and religious houses to replace what had been destroyed by fanaticism or war.

Thus, Rubens passed his adolescence in a city that was slowly but visibly taking a new lease on life. He studied first at the school of Rombout Verdonck, a scholar of some reputation, who continued the work that Jan Rubens had begun in shaping the boy's mind and taste. Here he made what was to be a lifelong friendship with Balthasar Moretus, a crippled boy a few years his senior. Moretus was the grandson of Christophe Plantin and would in time become the head of the famous printing press. "I knew him from his childhood," Moretus wrote in later years, "and I loved this young man who had the most perfect and the most amiable character."

Peter Paul's school days did not last long. In 1590 his sister Blandina was married, and the resources of the Rubens family were strained to provide her with a suitable dowry. As a result Philip, now 16, and Peter Paul, 13, set out to earn their living. Later, Maria Rubens was to note with some pride in her will: "From the time of my daughter's marriage my sons lived at their own cost." Philip, a promising scholar, was employed first as a clerk in the office of Jean Richardot, a prominent Netherlands statesman, and shortly after as tutor to his two sons. This meant that he accompanied them to the University of Louvain and was able to continue his own education while supervising theirs.

Things did not go so smoothly at first for Peter Paul. His mother placed him as page in the household of the Countess of Lalaing. This was a recognized route by which a young man of good family but limited means might make his way in the world. A well-behaved page could hope for promotion, as he grew older, to a responsible post with some nobleman and thence to a role in the affairs of the state. Thus did many a great political career begin. Rubens owed his polished manners and his familiarity with courtly ways to the time he spent with the Countess of Lalaing; but even then he knew that he wanted to be a painter, and after some months he persuaded his mother to remove him from the service of the Countess and apprentice him to an artist.

The traditional system of training in art still prevailed in the Netherlands. The postulant painter learned his craft, like any other apprentice, by manual labor in the workshop of a master, grinding and mixing the colors, preparing the canvases, cleaning his master's brushes and palette, meanwhile picking up what skill he could in drawing and painting from such instruction and advice as the master had time to give.

The choice of Rubens' first master, Tobias Verhaecht, seems to have been accidental, the result of a family connection: Verhaecht had recently married a relative of Maria Rubens. He was an unremarkable painter of small landscapes, for which there was a ready sale, and Rubens cannot have learned much from him. Very soon he transferred to the studio of the more versatile Adam van Noort, where he remained for about four years before moving again to attach himself, finally, to Otto van Veen, one of Antwerp's most distinguished painters.

Otto van Veen—or Vaenius as he liked to Latinize his name—had many good qualities. He was a man of learning and taste—one of the ablest members of Antwerp's elite group of "Romanists," painters who had studied in Italy and whose work was imbued with the humanist learning of the Renaissance. Vaenius' work was thoughtful, respectable —and almost lifeless. But he was nonetheless an important influence in the esthetic education of Rubens and well able to guide his pupil in the serious study of composition and to stimulate his interest in the intellectual aspects of their profession.

Vaenius was especially famous for his knowledge of symbols, those pictorial images by which abstract ideas could be visually expressed. Such symbols are now so little used in painting that few of us recognize more than a handful of them—the dove with an olive branch for Peace, the scales for Justice, the laurel for Victory. But in the 16th Century the propagation of ideas by symbols was an accepted function of art, whether popular or sophisticated. Saints, of course, were identified by their special attributes. St. Catherine had the wheel on which she was tortured, Mary Magdalen the jar of ointment with which she anointed Christ's feet, St. Jerome the lion he befriended in the desert. But even in portraits, allegories and other secular pictures, symbols were used to

The two woodcuts above, by the Swiss artist Tobias Stimmer, are scenes from his illustrated Bible, an extremely popular late 16th Century edition that strongly impressed the young Rubens. In copying elements of the Stimmer woodcuts, Rubens concentrated primarily on drawing the donkeys (below), foreshadowing a lifelong interest in painting animals in action.

convey a wordless commentary. Birds, flowers and animals were introduced into pictures with a purpose: the hare meant Vigilance, the cat Liberty, the serpent Wisdom; different flowers represented different virtues or, if their petals were dropping, stood for the ephemeral nature of youth and beauty.

Every artist had to understand the use of this kind of symbolism and there were many handbooks to explain it. The ingenious employment of symbols was much admired, and the educated public took pleasure in unraveling the meaning of these pictorial messages. This learned game gave interest and variety even to the most pedestrian works of art. In the hands of a man of genius it could be used to create visions of infinite diversity and delight. Throughout his life, Rubens' immense knowledge of symbols provided fuel for his imagination; he was never at a loss to translate his ideas (or those of his patrons) into an array of visual images. He laid the foundations for this knowledge in the studio of Vaenius, whom he admired and kept as a lifelong friend.

What other sources of artistic education was he exposed to during his formative years? His friendship with young Balthasar Moretus must have brought him into contact with publications in progress at the Plantin press, by then under the direction of Balthasar's father, the son-in-law and successor of the founder. There Rubens would have seen many nobly produced books, some with illustrations—for instance, a number of important botanical works with engraved plates. But the book that he recalled in later life as an early source of inspiration was not from the Plantin press. It was a celebrated picture Bible issued at Basel in 1576 with 170 woodcuts from the designs of an outstanding Swiss engraver of the time, Tobias Stimmer. One can imagine this book coming into the Rubens household perhaps as early as the Cologne days and awakening an immense excitement in the eager child. But this is conjecture. All that is known for certain is that Rubens was fascinated by Stimmer's illustrations when he was a student and that in his mature years he spoke of his debt to him.

At the age of 21, after seven or eight years as an apprentice, Rubens was accepted in 1598 as a master by the Guild of St. Luke, the Antwerp association of artists and artisans. Although he had as yet no studio of his own, and continued to work with Vaenius for another two years, he was now qualified to take pupils and he did have one, at least—Deodatus del Monte, son of an Antwerp silversmith.

Little is known of Rubens' work at this time. He must have been well thought of or he would not have had pupils. He must have been productive because it was his nature to be so. His mother obviously possessed a number of his paintings done during this period because she spoke of them proudly in her will. But there is only one signed work of these years, a highly finished portrait of a young man, the firmly modeled face vibrating with life.

Rubens was good, certainly. But he was not a young prodigy. He did not leap into instant fame, as the adolescent Anthony van Dyck was to do a few years later. There was nothing yet to startle and amaze his elders. He was still learning, acquiring what he could from the example of older Antwerp painters, but teaching himself more than they could teach him. Professionally he matured late, though not through any inherent slowness or lack of natural gifts—the quickness of his perceptions and assurance of his touch are apparent in the earliest drawings from his hand. It almost seems as though he deliberately held himself back through an astonishing capacity for self-discipline. Few painters with such evident talent have worked so long and so methodically at the foundations of their technique.

During Rubens' last year with Vaenius, the studio had an exciting contract on hand: the design for the reception at Antwerp of the new rulers of the Netherlands, the Archduke Albert and the Archduchess Isabella. From the days of the Dukes of Burgundy it had been the custom for the chief cities of the Netherlands to give their rulers a splendid civic welcome, called a *Joyeuse Entrée*. Triumphal arches spanned the street and young men and maidens in allegorical attire declaimed Latin speeches from richly adorned platforms or gilded chariots.

The important occasion for which Vaenius and his assistants were at work brought a promise of better times for the Netherlands. Shortly before his death in Madrid in 1598, Philip II had decided to grant political independence to the Spanish Netherlands, and to turn its rule over to Albert, an Austrian Habsburg prince, who was to marry Philip's favorite daughter, the Infanta Isabella. Actually the promised independence was more theoretical than real since the Netherlands remained a possession of the Habsburg family and in 1621 reverted to the Spanish crown. Culturally, however, the reign of Albert and Isabella was to be associated with a great revival. In this Golden Age—or more truly Golden Sunset —of Flemish art, Rubens played a leading part.

But when at the end of 1599 the royal pair entered Antwerp under the arches designed by Otto Vaenius, Rubens' youthful mind was fixed on other horizons. His master had studied in Italy; his father had spent seven years in Italy; his eldest brother Jan-Baptist, who can hardly have been more than a shadowy memory to Rubens, had died in Italy. Meanwhile, at the University of Louvain near Brussels, his beloved brother Philip had become the favorite pupil of the great humanist teacher Justus Lipsius, and was acquiring a reputation as a Classical scholar. Peter Paul must have been in frequent touch with Philip, seeking his advice and help, keeping up his Latin and stimulating his own interest in the world of antiquity. Inevitably he looked toward Rome, the Eternal City, the magnet for all artists and all scholars. Before he could achieve greatness as a painter—and it is safe to assume that Peter Paul had a healthy confidence in his own future—he must go to Italy.

Where the money came from is uncertain, but Rubens was always clever with money. Perhaps he sold some of his pictures; perhaps the father of his student Deodatus del Monte gave a little help, for Deodatus went with him on his travels. He did not need very much because, once he had arrived in Italy, he would be sure to find employment— Flemish painters were much admired there for landscapes. Whatever the background of that significant journey, it was in May 1600 that Peter Paul Rubens, aged not quite 23, set out for Italy.

Diplomat, Scholar, Artist

If the life of Peter Paul Rubens could be summed up in one word, that word would be energy. His art, characterized by vitality and passion, is the quintessence of the grandiose Baroque style. His more than 1,000 paintings constitute a monumental achievement. And this was only one of his many accomplishments.

Rubens was extremely well read, with interests ranging from Stoic philosophy to the study of rare gems. On his wide travels, during which he studiously examined and often copied the art of other eras, he met as an equal with some of Europe's foremost intellectuals. Among them were the Classical scholars Nicolas Peiresc and Caspar Scioppius and the French humanist Pierre Dupuy, all of whom praised his keen mind and engaged him in long and learned correspondence. But Rubens was no pedant. He had the skill and charm necessary for another undertaking—politics. For many years after he had become established as an artist, using his profession as a cover, Rubens worked as an effective diplomat, frequently participating in peace negotiations on behalf of his homeland, the Spanish Netherlands.

Despite this activity, Rubens found time for his family. He had the good fortune to marry two beautiful women (his first wife is shown at right), and was the devoted father of eight children. "Rubens had so many talents," said one of his patrons, "that his knowledge of painting should be considered the least of them."

Shortly after his first marriage in 1609, Rubens painted this portrait of himself and his bride. During their 17 years together, Isabella and the artist had three children and lived a harmonious and happy life in Antwerp. Upon Isabella's untimely death in 1626, Rubens was inconsolable.

The Artist and His Wife, Isabella Brant, in the Honeysuckle Bower, 1609

A Child's Head, c. 1618

The painting above is believed to be of Rubens' first child, Clara Serena, who died in 1623 at the age of 12. Her death was a terrible blow to the artist, who loved all his children dearly. Shortly after her death he painted his two sons *(right)*, perhaps in a grieving father's impulse to preserve his remaining children. In this remarkably sensitive double portrait, Albert, at the left, is pictured with a cocky smile, his legs crossed in the pose of a proper young gentleman, while Nicolas fixes his attention on a pet bird. Unlike earlier artists, who often made children look like miniature adults, Rubens evokes all the boyishness of his two robust youngsters.

The Artist's Sons, Albert and Nicolas, c. 1624-1625

Portrait of Philip IV, c. 1628-1629

Infanta Isabella Clara Eugenia, c. 1609

Archduke Albert, c. 1609

Portraits and Politics

Rubens' collected portraits comprise a virtual "Who's Who" of 17th Century nobility in Western Europe. During eight years in Italy he painted many aristocrats, including his earliest patron, the Duke of Mantua. In 1609, when he returned to Antwerp, he became court painter to the Archduke Albert and the Archduchess Isabella, Governors of the Spanish Netherlands —their portraits are seen at right—and in this capacity, he was privileged to visit among the rich and noble. He depicted King Charles I of England, the Duke of Buckingham, the Countess of Shrewsbury *(far right)*, King Philip IV of Spain *(top right)*, Kings Henry IV and Louis XIII of France, the Polish Prince Ladislas Sigismund, and Marie de' Medici, whose entire life he portrayed in a glorious series of paintings *(pages 109-119)*.

It was while traveling as a painter that Rubens engaged in his diplomatic activities. The Archduchess Isabella, realizing that Rubens' art afforded him entree into some of the principal ruling houses of Europe, made him her unofficial but trusted envoy. While he painted portraits and discussed commissions for larger decorative works for the walls of palaces, Rubens negotiated with kings and princes, often secretly, about the mutual interests of their two countries.

Some rulers were skeptical of this arrangement. In 1626, after Philip IV became King of Spain, he discovered that his aunt, Isabella, had entrusted peace negotiations with England to Rubens. Believing that a mere painter could not handle such a delicate situation, Philip objected. But Isabella, aware of Rubens' abilities, persisted, and the artist continued to serve Spain. Two years later when Rubens, again acting in a dual capacity, met the King in Madrid, Philip was able to see the charm, tact and intelligence that made the painter-diplomat such a valuable aide.

Alathea Talbot, Countess of Shrewsbury, 1620

49.

Titian: *Venus and Adonis*, 1554

22

Titian: *Self-Portrait*, 1566

A Debt to Titian

Of all the earlier painters of the past whom Rubens studied, the one who influenced him most was the 16th Century Venetian, Titian. When the young Rubens traveled to Italy he made numerous copies of Titian's work; later, as he began to acquire wealth, he purchased some of the Italian's originals. (After Rubens' death, 10 Titians were found in his home, among them the self-portrait at left above.)

Occasionally, when copying Titian's paintings, Rubens took the liberty of making changes. In Rubens' copy *(lower left)* of Titian's *Adam and Eve (center, left)* he added vitality and flow to the figures, while retaining the basic composition and color harmony. Rubens acknowledged his debt in many ways. He was especially inspired by Titian's use of color and choice of subject matter, both of which he freely adapted in many works, invested with his own sense of movement and energy. The style of Titian's *Venus and Adonis (far left)*, for example, is frequently echoed in Rubens' depictions of mythological subjects, large historical scenes and in his great nudes.

Curiously, the parallels between Titian and Rubens do not end with their artistic styles. Both were prolific painters of religious and mythological subjects; both designed engravings, and both were sought as portraitists. In addition, each artist mingled freely with the nobles and intellectuals of his time, and each had an extremely rich and successful career. Finally, they stand together as fountainheads of the tradition of brilliant color in painting; they are invariably cited by such later masters of color as Watteau, Delacroix, Cézanne and Matisse.

Titian: *Adam and Eve*, c. 1570

Rubens: *Adam and Eve*, c. 1628-29

23

GALLERIA PITTI, FLORENCE

The Four Philosophers, c. 1612-1614

Besides painting and politics, Rubens was greatly interested in Classical studies. His *Four Philosophers* *(above)* documents this penchant. In it, he portrayed *(from right to left)* the scholar Jan Woverius, the renowned Stoic philosopher Justus Lipsius, Rubens' brother Philip—Lipsius' disciple—and Rubens himself.

In the gallery and museum of his home in Antwerp *(right)*—a popular attraction for intellectuals and nobility visiting the Spanish Netherlands—Rubens displayed his magnificent collection of paintings and sculptures, a remarkable array of antique gems, coins and medals, and an extensive library of ancient and contemporary books.

24

Rubens was well paid for his art, and in 1610 he purchased a large house in Antwerp. During his first trip to Italy he had been fascinated with the architecture, and when he added a studio *(at left in the large photograph)* he designed an Italianate façade. It is decorated with Classical sculpture, inscriptions from Roman literature and Baroque stonework. Rubens was so enamored of this style that he published a book on Genoese architecture to inspire others to build such houses. After his death, the house was sold, and in succeeding hands much of the interior was changed. However, in 1939, the city of Antwerp began restoring the edifice and now visitors can see this elegant home much as it was when Rubens was alive.

A bedroom

A dining room

The Rubens home in Antwerp

II

The Impact of Italy

When Peter Paul Rubens started on his journey to Italy he was better prepared than most young painters who had crossed the Alps before him. He already spoke Italian, probably learned from his father in early youth. He also read and wrote Latin with ease and was familiar with most of the great writers of antiquity.

By June 1600 he was in Venice. That opulent city, the Queen of the Adriatic, had passed the zenith of its glory, but there was as yet little outward sign of decay. Architecture and the decorative arts flourished and the quays were busier than were those of Antwerp. One imagines the young Rubens exploring the narrow alleys between the high houses, pausing on the stepped bridges over the canals in delighted enjoyment of each new perspective that opened before him in the watery light, entering churches and public buildings to examine with attentive pleasure the carved doorways and gilded ceilings, monumental tombs, rich hangings and the glowing works of the Venetian masters of the previous century.

Titian, the greatest of these painters, had died in 1576, the year before Rubens was born. His fame, which had reached all Europe while he lived, was still bright. The admiration that Rubens felt for him was to increase as the Flemish painter matured. Titian's sumptuous coloring, his strong yet fluid line, his mastery of form and the power of his imagination impressed Rubens ever more deeply as the years went by. Eventually, he acquired nine paintings by Titian for his own collection and made copies of more than 30 others, and at the height of his own fame he saluted Titian with reverence and love as the greatest of all masters.

But as a young man seeing the splendors of Venetian painting for the first time, Rubens was more influenced by the works of Tintoretto and Veronese. In room after room of the Doges' Palace in Venice he saw walls and ceilings that these celebrated painters had gorgeously enhanced with Christian visions and pagan allegories, with tributes to the might of Venice and with scenes from its past history. On the wall of the Sala del Gran Consiglio (the Great Council Hall) the aged Tintoretto and his son had recently completed what is still one of the largest paintings in the world, measuring 72 by 23 feet. It is a shimmering vision of Para-

This chalk drawing by Rubens is based on one of Michelangelo's male nudes on the Sistine Chapel ceiling. A careful copy, although somewhat more sensuous than the original, it is one of many studies that Rubens made of Italian paintings and sculpture.

Drawing after Michelangelo, c. 1601-1608

dise, where myriads of the Blessed in ever-widening arcs gaze toward the Savior and the Virgin enthroned in shining light.

Rubens studied the work of Tintoretto also in the spacious halls of the Scuola di San Rocco, a Venetian guild hall, observing the master's use of transverse shafts of light across dark shadows. He especially noted in the great *Crucifixion* the figures straining to lift the Cross. It was six years since Tintoretto had died. But his studio had been a family business—his sons, his son-in-law and at least one daughter working with him—and when Rubens was there the business still went on, captained by Tintoretto's son Domenico. Using the innumerable studies and drawings left by the master, the family still concocted passable imitations—and continued to do so for another 50 years. Rubens can hardly have failed to visit so interesting a workshop. He would have seen there not only the vast store of drawings—a whole vocabulary of expressive gestures, faces, attitudes ready to be copied as the need served for large works—but also Tintoretto's sketches in paint, lightning first ideas of genius, swift massings of form and light for some great design.

Rubens was no less attracted by the airy and brilliant paintings of Veronese that enriched the Church of San Sebastiano. Many years later they would provide him with inspiration when he came to decorate the ceiling of the Jesuit church in Antwerp and the King of England's huge Banqueting House in London.

Rubens' stay in Venice was cut short by an opportunity he could not afford to refuse. In July 1600, Vincenzo I, Duke of Mantua, a small duchy in Northern Italy, stopped in Venice on his way home from a visit to Northern Europe. Vincenzo was an ambitious, licentious prince who spent lavish sums indulging his taste for beautiful women and magnificent display. But he also had important redeeming qualities. As a patron of arts, music and letters, he was genuinely sympathetic to men of talent. He cherished and encouraged the superb musical gifts of Monteverdi, and as a young man he had been instrumental in securing the release of the poet Tasso from the madhouse and restoring him to normal life.

Vincenzo had visited Antwerp on his northern journey and may have heard something of Rubens, though there is no record of it. At any rate, so the story goes, one of the Duke's attendant gentlemen met Rubens at his inn in Venice, fell into talk with him and looked at his sketches. Impressed, he showed them to the Duke, who at once engaged the artist to go with him to Mantua.

The service of the Duke offered great advantages, but at the price of some servitude. Princely patrons did not support young painters solely to enable them to cultivate their talents. Rubens had to work for his keep. At first his task was to make copies of famous pictures for the Duke's collection, to paint portraits of pretty women for the Gallery of Beauties that Vincenzo, following a contemporary fashion, was organizing at Mantua, and to design pageants and festivities for the court. More interesting commissions might follow but there was no certainty of that.

Yet the opportunities far outweighed the burdens. The young painter could travel all over Italy to see the best pictures; the Duke very soon gave him permission to make his own choice of masterpieces worth copying for the collection. Besides reaping the benefits of this subsidized tour of Renaissance art, a painter working for so august a nobleman would become known to other patrons; loyalty to his employer was expected within reason, but it was permissible to build up other connections by taking commissions that did not interfere with his service to the Duke.

Rubens' attachment to the ducal suite began in October 1600 with a journey to Florence for one of the most notable weddings of the age. The bride, Marie de' Medici, was the younger sister of Vincenzo's wife. The groom was the King of France. The King could not find the time to come to his own wedding, and the ceremony was conducted by proxy; nonetheless, the occasion was a magnificent one, and it also offered Rubens an opportunity, between festivities, to see the wonders of Florence.

It is possible that he painted the royal bride for the Duke's Gallery of Beauties. She was a buxom blonde with the one attribute Rubens admired above all others in women—a beautiful skin. At any rate, he attended the wedding banquet and was delighted with the lavish arrangements, which included a fanciful rainbow over the banquet table and a girl, dressed as Athena, who sang most beautifully. His vivid memory of the event was to be useful to him decades later when the bride—by then a widow and queen dowager of France—gave him one of his largest commissions, the task of decorating her Parisian palace with the story of her life.

But in 1600 Rubens was still a beginner, zealously visiting the sights of Florence, such as Michelangelo's stupendous tombs for the Medici in the Church of San Lorenzo, and admiring the works of the leading Florentine painters. The most distinguished of these then at work in the city was Ludovico Cigoli. In the perspective of time Rubens is a giant in comparison, but Cigoli was significant in his day for having the vision to break free from the overweighty influence of Michelangelo and the mannerisms that had dominated Italian painting for the previous 50 years. Cigoli's painting was not entirely free of the past, of course, but it was a departure from the contorted affectation of Mannerist art, and in its direct expression of emotion it foreshadowed a basic element of the Baroque style. Rubens respectfully studied Cigoli's work, especially his altarpieces, and was impressed by its calm dignity.

More important even than the influence of the art of Florence was the effect of the art Rubens saw and lived with in Mantua. The principal glory of the ducal palace itself was the superb collection of art accumulated by the Duke and his ancestors from every part of Italy. No other collection in Europe at that time offered so wide a range for study. Here were the great processional paintings of the Paduan master Mantegna, who had been court painter to a 15th Century ancestor of Vincenzo; here were magical canvases by Correggio, works by Titian and Raphael and by Raphael's most famous pupil, Giulio Romano, who 60 years earlier had served as chief artist to Vincenzo's grandfather. In 1600 it was a truism of art that Raphael represented the ultimate ideal. So Rubens, working for the same noble family that had employed Giulio, and living among his works, must have felt at only one remove from the supreme master.

As an artist in his own right, Giulio had been one of the acknowledged masters of Europe and a creator of the Mannerist style that grew out of

On one of his first visits to Rome, Rubens was so intrigued by figures on the end of a sarcophagus (*above*) that he sketched them (*below*). Obviously, the head of the central figure interested him most, for he drew it twice, giving the old man's face a critical expression as he looks at the woman at right. Rubens scribbled an amusing note on the sketch, identifying the man and his peevish wife: "Socrates, no doubt, and Xanthippe, whom he cannot endure."

the High Renaissance. Indeed, such was his reputation that he has the distinction of being the only artist mentioned by Shakespeare (in *The Winter's Tale,* Act V, Scene 2). Giulio was responsible for the creation of one of the outstanding works of the Mannerist period, the ducal summer house in Mantua called the Palazzo del Te. This low-lying building, with its open loggias and ingeniously planned vistas, stood (and still stands) as a monument to the technical skill and varied invention of its creator, who not only designed it but also decorated it with paintings that display a strong imagination and immense energy. In these works, Giulio added to the tradition of Raphael something poetic and bizarre, even a kind of fury of his own. *The Fall of the Titans* in the Palazzo del Te is an avalanche of thrashing limbs and grotesque, enormous faces trapped in an earthquake of hurtling rocks and fractured columns.

Rubens was unquestionably influenced by Giulio's work. In Venice he had first seen the splendor of painted ceilings; in Mantua he could observe at leisure the work that had earned Giulio a reputation as one of the greatest decorators of the previous century. Rubens could learn much from a study of Giulio's solutions to the problems of pictorial design, applied to large wall spaces complicated by the interior architecture of windows, doorways, domes and spandrels. Thirty-six years later, when the King of Spain commissioned Rubens to decorate his pleasure palace and hunting lodge, the Torre de la Parada near Madrid, the artist's thoughts reverted to the paintings in the Palazzo del Te. Here and there in the huge series of mythological scenes he designed for the Spanish King, figures and themes from Giulio Romano appeared transmuted.

Rubens' self-educational travels around Italy in the service of the Duke continued for eight years. Although his movements cannot be traced exactly, he went to Florence and Genoa, Pisa, Padua and Verona, Lucca and Parma, more than once to Venice, perhaps to Urbino, and certainly to Milan, where he made a sketch of Leonardo da Vinci's *Last Supper.* He also stayed twice for long periods in Rome. Very few painters in any epoch have known Italy as fully as Rubens came to know it. His letters home during this period are written in lively and accurate Italian and signed "Pietro Pauolo," the form he adhered to for the rest of his life. (Though his mother called him Peter, he seems to have resisted all other attempts to use his first name alone.)

Rubens' first major journey was to Rome, where the Duke, well pleased with his performance as a copyist, sent him to reproduce some pictures in the collection of Cardinal Alessandro Montalto. It was thus in the summer of 1601 that Rubens first entered the Eternal City: grand, corrupt, incomparable, heart of Catholic Christendom, center of Classical studies, artistic capital of the world.

It is hardly possible now to convey what Rome at the height of the Catholic revival must have meant to a man like Rubens—an ardent Catholic, a devotee of Classical antiquity, and an impressionable young painter.

An extraordinary upsurge in ecclesiastical building and decoration had been inspired by the spiritual renewal of the Church and by the demands of a religion that aimed to attract attention and excite devotion by every visual means. The new style in architecture that shaped this activity (the label "Baroque" was not actually applied until very much later) had begun with the building of the magnificent church of the Jesuits, the Gesù, consecrated in 1584. A vast hall, not divided by pillars, provided both an open setting for processions and the largest possible auditorium for sermons and for ritual worship. An airy dome illuminated by wide windows let in a flood of light from on high and drew the eyes of the faithful toward the heavens, while quiet and privacy could be found in small side chapels along the huge open nave.

This was a key design for many European churches of the future, a design basically simple but one that offered great opportunities for elaborate embellishment. Around the high altar, in the side chapels, in the dome itself, artists were called upon to enhance with painting and sculpture the impression of an upward-looking faith.

While new churches were being built and older churches enlarged and beautified in accordance with the new theories of design, Michelangelo's great dome of St. Peter's—which had been completed in 1590—dominated the city, rising majestically above the still-unfinished basilica and outsoaring the tall Egyptian obelisk that had recently been erected in the half-planned piazza before it.

Actually, the zealous Catholic reform of the Counter Reformation had at first opposed rather than embraced the arts. Pope Paul IV was with difficulty dissuaded from destroying Michelangelo's gigantic nudes in the Sistine Chapel. It was also credibly reported that El Greco had offered to repaint the entire ceiling in a style more suited to a sacred building.

But gradually the esthetic views of the Catholic Church became less austere. Artists were no longer discouraged from studying the antique statues that had been considered relics of a pagan past in the Vatican galleries, and their work was increasingly in demand for the decoration of churches. The purpose of this decoration was not only to glorify God but to educate the worshipers. In this there was a return to the ideas that had inspired medieval craftsmen: pictures and sculpture were to tell a story and point a moral. Rules were laid down for the artist to follow: treatment of religious themes was to be easily comprehensible to the faithful, and realistic within limits, but still reverent and uplifting.

In creating this vibrant new art, Rubens' Italian contemporaries frequently made use of figures taken from the work of other painters or copied from statues and reliefs. The quest for originality that has come to dominate creative art in modern times played little part in their thinking. Although they were capable of breaking away from the forms and ideas of the past, they regarded the masterpieces of the previous century and the rediscovered masterpieces of Classical sculpture as a sort of treasury of ideas on which they could draw.

Rubens must have spent hours twisting his neck in the Sistine Chapel to study the superb poses of Michelangelo's figures. Other more comfortable hours were doubtless passed in the Stanze of the Vatican, the incomparable series of apartments decorated by Raphael, or down by the Tiber in the elegant halls of the Villa Farnesina copying Raphael's enchanting visual ballet of Cupid and Psyche. Rubens' ambition, like that of other young artists of his time, was not to find a new way of seeing things but to find new ways of using the great discoveries of his predecessors. First he had to learn from them everything that their works could teach him about form and color and technique. A part of his future greatness lay in his immense capacity for synthesizing disparate influences, ancient or modern, into a new vision of his own. The secret of this vision, of his own peculiar genius, was his vibrating sense of life and movement.

Of all the influences shaping the course of Italian art at this time, perhaps the most turbulent was that of Caravaggio—most difficult of men and most controversial of painters—who was at the height of his fame when Rubens reached Rome. Caravaggio came from Northern Italy and was only four years older than Rubens. A violent, feckless, impulsive man, and a painter of precocious genius who fought his way up through poverty and neglect, he now enjoyed impressive patronage in Rome. Rubens knew his pictures but it is unlikely that he ever met the painter. Caravaggio had a reputation for ferocious and irregular conduct, and was frequently involved in fights and duels. His personality would not have appealed to the polite and well-behaved Rubens, nor would the egotistical Caravaggio have taken the slightest interest in an unknown Flemish artist employed to copy pictures for the Duke of Mantua.

Nevertheless, Rubens was impressed by Caravaggio's paintings and even copied some of them. The Italian innovator was a master in the use of chiaroscuro, the dramatic balance of light and shadow, to highlight his figures, to suggest textures and define surfaces. But the most striking aspect of Caravaggio's work was its realism, which went beyond anything most painters of the day had attempted. Instead of idealizing Biblical figures in his religious pictures, Caravaggio modeled them on actual people, as in his *Deposition of Christ,* in which the faces of the three Marys and of Nicodemus have clearly been drawn from life. In one picture, *St. Matthew and the Angel,* painted for a church, Caravaggio portrayed St. Matthew with a plebeian face and coarse, unshapely feet. Such treatment often shocked and offended contemporary critics. The *St. Matthew* had to be painted again, and several other commissioned works were rejected by patrons who felt his realism had gone too far. But the Caravaggesque blend of realism and chiaroscuro was powerful enough to have an effect on the art of 17th Century painters all over Europe.

Rubens admired Caravaggio's work but he had some reservations about it. He particularly did not care for the Italian's technique, which seemed to Rubens to be labored and slow. This opinion, which Rubens rendered retrospectively when he was himself a famous man, is very revealing. During his long years of self-imposed study Rubens was trying to work out and perfect a technique that would enable him to keep pace with the speed of his ideas—the technique that ultimately enabled him to paint faster and more fluently than, probably, any other painter has ever done.

He recognized a technique that was much closer than Caravaggio's to what he needed when he studied the works of another celebrated Italian painter. This was the Bolognese master, Annibale Carracci, who was working in Rome on his superb decoration of the Farnese Palace. Carracci had developed a method of rapidly sketching from life in chalk that Rubens was quick to imitate. Stylistically Carracci was quite different

Rubens improved his drawing skill not only by copying the work of others but in some cases by applying his own pen or brush directly to their work. To an unfinished engraving by Cornelius Cort, showing the *Penitent St. Jerome,* he added, with softer brushstrokes in brown ink, an entire landscape, including the broad-brimmed hat and crumpled cloak at right. Rubens collected sketches and engravings wherever he went, and a number of the other items in his huge collection also bear the mark of his busy hand.

from Caravaggio; his conceptions were Classical in line and composed with a sculptural dignity that strongly reflected traditional elements—an expression that Rubens found congenial with his own artistic approach.

There was also a lively colony of North European artists in Rome, mostly engaged in landscape painting. One of these, the German etcher and painter Adam Elsheimer, was almost the same age as Rubens and became a close friend. He painted small, carefully wrought pictures of mysterious beauty—*The Flight into Egypt, Landscape with St. John the Baptist Preaching*—landscapes with figures often illuminated by moonlight or by torchlight. Rubens was enthralled by the delicate intensity of his friend's vision, though his own painting aimed at larger and more ambitious effects.

Actually, very little of Rubens' work of the early years in Italy still exists. But recently one picture, *The Judgment of Paris,* has come to light that appears to date from this time. Intoxicated by the splendors of antique sculpture and Renaissance painting, the young painter attempted in this work rather more than he could manage. It is a large picture and the three opulent, naked goddesses lined up for their beauty contest are somewhat overwhelming. The organization of the figures is original but a little awkward. The landscape, however, has a poetic quality, and the very faults of the picture indicate Rubens' latent, still undeveloped capacities.

Rubens had not been in Rome long when he received an important commission. The Netherlands' Archduke Albert, for whose reception in Antwerp Rubens had helped design triumphal arches, had been criticized at the Vatican for lack of religious zeal. To counteract this, he instructed his representative in Rome to commission at his expense three altarpieces for the chapel of St. Helena in the Church of Santa Croce in Gerusalemme. The Archduke's representative was the eldest son of the Flemish statesman Jean Richardot, who had employed Philip Rubens as tutor to his sons. Naturally, the commission was offered to Philip's brother.

It was a fine opportunity for Rubens, and an inspiring task—his first important commission for a church. The work still exists; though it has suffered much with the passage of time, it still displays the imaginative power and technical skill that the painter brought to his task. Over the center altar Rubens painted St. Helena herself, a queenly figure in gold brocade. Over the right altar he showed Christ crowned with thorns, over the left the elevation of the Cross.

The *Crown of Thorns* in particular reveals the exceptional quality of Rubens' visual imagination and that sense of the movement and continuity of life that was to be typical of his mature work. The figure of Christ in the center recalls a work by Titian on the same subject, but is borrowed more directly from two famous Greek statues, the *Torso of Belvedere* and the *Laocoön.* Rubens borrowed only the outward shape; the spirit was his own, and every line of face and body tells of the exhausted immobility of pain. The soldiers, in contrast, are all nervous activity. As a young painter on his mettle, Rubens showed his skill in, for example, an effective contrast between the lantern light of the foreground and the moonlight of the background. But the picture is memorable less for such displays of technical skill than for the tragic expressiveness of the central figure.

After the Santa Croce commission, Rubens returned to Mantua, and

Sometimes Rubens retouched other artists' drawings that were in his possession so thoroughly that they almost became his own works. This drawing, made in 1530 by David Hopfer, originally showed the woman behind the shield. Rubens, apparently for his own amusement, redrew her in front of it. A fold of the skirt, which Rubens added, roughly follows the original outline of the left side of the shield. Rubens also altered the face, hat and parts of the shield, leaving only the architecture as it had been.

in March of 1603 was entrusted by the Duke with the responsible mission of taking a number of presents to the King of Spain. (Spanish influence was considerable in Northern Italy, and it behooved the head of a small state to keep in the King's good graces.) The gifts consisted of a beautifully wrought small carriage and six horses, some interesting new firearms, precious perfumes and a score of pictures copied—not by Rubens—from famous originals in Rome. These latter were intended as a flattering gift to the Duke of Lerma, chief minister and favorite of the King, who claimed to be a patron of the arts. Rubens was to superintend the transport of the gifts and to see them duly presented to the King and his minister.

The journey to Spain was far from easy. It involved mountainous roads and a long sea passage, and Rubens had been given inadequate funds and equipment. Floods in Florence held up the journey for some days, and then there was difficulty in getting a ship from Leghorn to the Spanish port of Alicante. Before setting sail Rubens reported his progress to Mantua: "The horses, the men and the baggage are on board ship; we now need only a favorable wind. . . . We have taken provisions for one month and paid the charges. . . . The expenses for the horses are large but necessary, including wine-baths and other costly things."

A few weeks later he was able to report his arrival at the Spanish court with the presents intact, "the horses sleek and handsome"—as indeed they ought to have been after their beauty treatment in wine. But fresh trouble arose when the pictures were taken out of their cases: "The pictures . . . were discovered today . . . to be so damaged and spoiled that I almost despair of being able to restore them. . . . The canvas . . . is entirely rotted . . . (even though it was protected by a tin casing and a double oilcloth and packed in a wooden chest). The deterioration is . . . due to the continuous rains, which lasted for twenty-five days—an incredible thing in Spain."

Fortunately the pictures dried out better than Rubens had anticipated. He put right most of the damage by some deft repainting, and he substituted an original work of his own for two that were beyond repair.

The Duke of Mantua's representative at the Spanish court, a formal and self-important man, undertook personally to present the gifts intended for the King. He did allow Rubens, however, to assist in presenting the pictures to the Duke of Lerma. The Duke surveyed them with satisfaction, taking the copies for originals; Rubens was too tactful to enlighten him. Furthermore, Rubens' own picture came in for praise. Within a short while he received a dazzling commission to paint an equestrian portrait of the Duke himself.

With this picture, Rubens, now 26 years old, rose to full stature. He chose to represent the Duke in the most difficult manner possible, riding toward the spectator. This involved, first, a difficult feat of perspective, and, secondly, a yet more difficult problem of composition. In an equestrian portrait in profile the rider naturally dominates the horse; but if the horse is shown advancing toward the spectator, the striking image of the animal can easily eclipse the smaller figure of the man in the saddle. Rubens solved the problem in a strong and well-balanced composition, using, perhaps for the first time, a dominating upward spiral, which was so often to be a feature of his design. The eye is carried smoothly from the graceful curve of the horse's neck up to the military figure of the rider.

The Duke of Lerma had never been remarkable for brains and his once-handsome face had grown heavy and slack. But a man who has been, however incompetently, at the head of a great state for several years acquires a kind of wary dignity, an air at least of thoughtfulness if not of wisdom. Such a look Rubens gave to the face of Lerma. The portrait was well received by the sitter and admired by the Spanish court. Within a few years its fame had spread abroad, inspiring other painters to attempt the same design.

Such an achievement made Rubens impatient of the Duke of Mantua's continual requests for portraits of pretty women. In a cautiously phrased letter he asked to be excused from going to France to paint the French court beauties, but he does seem to have obediently painted some of the Spanish ladies during the remainder of his stay in Spain.

On his way back to Mantua, Rubens stopped in Genoa, a city he was to visit frequently in the next years to paint a number of portraits of some of the city's wealthy patricians. In these commissions Rubens showed the versatility with which he could turn from religious painting to secular subjects such as portraits and mythological themes. Of the latter, few survive from his Italian years, though there is one, a wild, strangely romantic *Hero and Leander,* that seems to date from this period.

A year after his return from Spain, Rubens achieved his first flawless success in a religious work, with a picture for the high altar of the Jesuit church in Genoa. Rubens was often in later life to work for the Jesuits, whose crusading faith and disciplined devotion strongly attracted him. In his picture of the *Circumcision* for their altar, Rubens once again combined ideas from other painters. There is an impetuous upward surge of the composition, which he derived from Correggio's paintings in the cathedral at Parma; from Correggio too he took the idea of portraying the Infant as though the light proceeds from Him. The richness and massing of the color owed much to Titian. The noble figure of the Virgin was based on a Roman statue.

But all the borrowings, all the influences were this time molded into a vision that was Rubens' own. The Virgin combines the realism of feeling with the idealization of form on which the Church insisted. She holds herself with Classical dignity, but turns her head away, in human distress, from the pain her Child has to suffer. Her gesture of withdrawal carries the eye of the spectator upward from the concentration of dark human forms around the tiny shining Child to the burst of celestial light and the throng of angels above. It is a supreme expression in art of the ideals of the era's Catholic Christendom: the human world and the heavenly world, the seen and the unseen, indissolubly linked by a divine sacrifice. This beautiful picture made it clear, for the first time, how perfectly the inspiration of Rubens reflected the religious spirit of his age.

Sometime in the spring of 1605 Rubens must have had news from his learned brother Philip in the Netherlands. Philip had already come to Italy once, but now a second visit was in prospect. Philip's reputation stood so high in the world of learning that it was generally assumed he

A preliminary sketch by Rubens for his equestrian portrait of the Spanish Duke of Lerma shows the difficulty of the task the artist set himself. He wanted the massive form of the horse to lend drama to his composition, without the animal dominating his subject. So he focused attention on the rider by means of the upward curve of the horse's front leg, neck and head. In the finished painting, Rubens filled the upper portion with swirling branches and a darkening sky that further draw the viewer's eye toward the Duke's face.

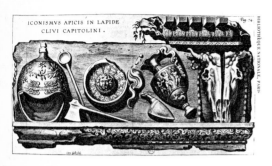

A copy of a bas-relief, above, showing paraphernalia of the priests of Jupiter, was one of many engravings designed by Rubens to illustrate a book on ancient Rome by his brother Philip. The brothers spent two years together in Rome touring the city and studying ancient statues, friezes and tombs.

The engraving above is after a Rubens study of toga drapery copied from a statue of the Emperor Titus. Below is a frieze depicting a chariot race, which has just been started by the *praetor* at left. The brothers' book, which dealt with many aspects of Roman society, was published in Antwerp in 1608.

would inherit the professorial chair of his famous teacher Justus Lipsius at the University of Louvain. But his yearning to return to Italy compelled him to relinquish this opportunity just as it was within his grasp. Armed with a letter of introduction from Lipsius which secured him the post of librarian to Cardinal Ascanio Colonna, he journeyed to Rome. Rubens persuaded his accommodating employer that he needed a refresher course in Rome and in the fall of 1605 the brothers set up house with two servants in the Via della Croce near the Piazza de Spagna.

Rubens' second sojourn in Rome was much longer than the first. It lasted, with occasional interruptions, for nearly three years, which were spent for the most part in intensive study both of painting and of antiquities. In Philip's company, Peter Paul acquired an expert knowledge of ancient Rome. His interests ranged from antique gems to contemporary architecture, from the careful drawing of Classical statues to rapid sketches from life, from the sophisticated interior decoration of Roman palaces to the pastoral landscape of the countryside surrounding Rome and the romantic ruins of the Palatine Hill. He developed his excellent mental and visual memory and, by incessant discipline and practice, acquired a speed and assurance in drawing that has rarely been equaled.

While he made careful studies of statues, both antique and more recent, learning everything that these could teach him about the human form, he was always acutely conscious of the pitfalls of this method. In later life he was to admonish young artists against the dangers of copying statues too slavishly. The painter, he said, must always bear in mind the difference between the two arts, and not copy peculiarities of treatment that arise merely from the nature of the sculptor's material and technique. The copying of sculpture, Rubens warned, will have a deadening effect on the style of an artist who fails to make these adjustments. Rubens himself was in no such danger. With his abounding vitality, he endowed every statue with life so that his drawings often seem to go back beyond the stone or bronze to the living model.

He demonstrated this gift in a project he undertook jointly with his brother. Philip was at work on a study of Roman customs and social life. Peter Paul, with typical enthusiasm, set out to illustrate his brother's text with details of Roman statues. Even these essentially scholarly drawings have a life of their own. Turning the pages of this handsome book, which Balthasar Moretus published a few years later at the Plantin press in Antwerp, one seems to be looking at senators and matrons of flesh and blood rather than at their cold images.

At about this time, Rubens experienced some anxiety about his friend Adam Elsheimer, who was having neurotic difficulty in finishing his pictures and was running into debt. Caravaggio, meanwhile, had blasted his Roman career by killing a man in a brawl. To escape arrest he fled— and was to die three years later, shipwrecked and stranded in a small port in Tuscany. He left behind him in Rome his great *Death of the Virgin,* which had been rejected by his patrons because the corpse was too realistic. (It was rumored Caravaggio had used as a model the body of a woman who had drowned in the Tiber.) Rubens, who deeply admired the work, persuaded the Duke of Mantua to buy it. Later, he arranged the purchase of another Caravaggio painting for a church in Antwerp.

In the autumn of 1606 he received, probably through the intervention of one of his Genoese patrons, one of the most coveted commissions in Rome—the main altarpiece for the newly built church of the Oratorians, Santa Maria in Vallicella, or, as the Romans call it to this day, La Chiesa Nuova, the New Church. The task was not simple. The space for the altarpiece was tall and narrow, and the Oratorian fathers wanted no fewer than six saints in the picture.

They could not have found a more obliging painter than Rubens. His studies of ancient Rome gave him a particular interest in this commission because some of the saints to be depicted were martyrs—among them St. Domitilla, a noble lady and niece of a Roman emperor—whose purported relics had been recently found in excavations of the catacombs. Rubens took special care in painting these saints, showing Pope Gregory the Great in splendid glowing vestments, and portraying St. Domitilla as a regal figure in shimmering satin with pearls in her golden hair. He was deeply disappointed, when the altarpiece was set in place, to find that the reflections caused by bad lighting made it almost invisible. He satisfied the Oratorians by painting a new altarpiece on slate to minimize reflections, and he took back the original work.

Philip Rubens went home to Antwerp in the summer of 1607 and Peter Paul stayed behind in Italy, spending some weeks in attendance on the Duke of Mantua at the summer resort of San Pier d'Arena near Genoa. But his steadily growing reputation had made its way back to the Netherlands. From Antwerp the Archduke Albert addressed a letter to Vincenzo asking him to permit his Flemish painter to return home. The Duke saw no reason to do so and it is doubtful whether Rubens himself at this time wished to leave Italy. He was thinking of settling there permanently, as so many northern artists had done.

On the other hand, his relations with the Duke were not altogether satisfactory. Vincenzo had been on the whole a generous and considerate employer and Rubens was always in later years to speak of him with gratitude, though criticizing him as a ruler and as a man for his political judgment and senseless extravagance, which had weakened the state of Mantua. But after eight years of service, Rubens may have felt that the Duke undervalued him. For instance, Vincenzo had never bought a single Rubens work for his own collection, though Rubens' pictures had been bought by other connoisseurs in Genoa and Rome. In fact, when Rubens suggested that the Duke should acquire the altarpiece he had withdrawn from the Chiesa Nuova—Rubens felt it was easily his best work—Vincenzo was not interested.

Then in the autumn of 1608 Rubens had news from Antwerp that his mother was seriously ill. Without waiting for the Duke's permission, without waiting for the unveiling of his new altarpiece at the Chiesa Nuova, he set out on the long journey home. He did not intend to stay long; he told the Duke's steward that he looked forward to his return. His heart, his life, his career—all seemed to belong to Italy.

Yet, when on October 28, 1608, the Duke of Mantua's Flemish painter rode out of Rome, it was for the last time.

Creator of Baroque

Few artists, however great, can be credited with the invention of a new style. Rubens is one of the exceptions. He created the vivid, dramatic mode of expression that was later called Baroque. The unique qualities of his innovation are particularly evident in the transitional early work shown at the right. The woman on the left is stiffly posed and painted in the highly detailed manner that was characteristic of Rubens' predecessors. But the heroic figure of the knight and his rearing horse, the animated gestures and brilliant colors demonstrate Rubens' new interest in violent action, movement and emotion. Paintings such as this anticipated by some 20 years the widespread adoption of the Baroque style by artists in other European countries.

Rubens' flamboyant Baroque style is characterized by large, heavy figures in active motion and an excited emotional atmosphere. Strong contrasts of light and shadow, and warm, rich colors infuse his paintings with energy. He painted robust Biblical scenes, tumultuous animal hunts, clashing battle scenes and powerful evocations of the religious spirit, all with equal dedication to high drama. One of his greatest admirers, the 19th Century French colorist, Eugène Delacroix, wrote of Rubens: "His principal quality, if one may be preferred among so many, is a prodigious spirit, that is to say, a prodigious life; without it, no artist is really great. . . . Titian and Paul Veronese are tame beside him."

Many painters before Rubens had been charmed by the legend of St. George, the knight who saved a princess by slaying a ferocious dragon. A familiar Christian allegory, the story especially suited the devout Rubens. Moreover, it satisfied his taste for picturing violent action and lovely women.

St. George and the Dragon, c. 1606-1610

41

Old Testament stories frequently provided Rubens with material for the sweeping pictorial spectacles that he loved. From *Adam and Eve in Paradise* to *Daniel in the Lions' Den*, Rubens found the Bible filled with subjects that not only suited his temperament and style but pleased his patrons as well.

One of his most exciting Biblical pictures *(left)* is based on the chapters from Isaiah that tell the story of King Sennacherib, whose Assyrian warriors had conquered all the cities of Judah and were now bent on assaulting the holy city of Jerusalem. But Jerusalem, they found, was a far more difficult problem than the others, for it was ruled by King Hezekiah, who had newly repledged his faith in God. The result, as told in Isaiah, is the subject of the painting: "Then the angel of the Lord went forth and smote in the camp of the Assyrians a hundred and four score and five thousand: and when they arose early in the morning, behold, they were all dead corpses."

Rubens may have found the Biblical text a bit too tame, for he took a few liberties in painting it. Rather than picture the slaughter of warriors sleeping in their camp, the artist showed them mounted, their battle ranks dissolving in chaos. Not merely one but a host of the Lord's avenging messengers swoop down from a violent sky broken by brilliant shafts of heavenly light. The turbaned King Sennacherib is seen to the left of center as he falls screaming from his terrified horse.

Rubens was particularly fond of the dismounted-rider motif, in which the vigorous S-shaped curve of the rearing horse serves as counterpoint to the diagonal of the falling man. He repeated it in a number of other paintings, two of which appear on following pages.

The Defeat of Sennacherib, 1616-1618

An opportunity to illustrate dramatic scenes from the Classical past was provided Rubens when, in 1617, he was asked by a group of Genoese noblemen to design a series of tapestries recording the highlights in the life of a famous consul of ancient Roman times, Decius Mus. Basing his pictures on descriptions that he read in Livy's *Histories,* Rubens produced six huge oil paintings, the most striking of which is shown above. In the tumultuous

Victory and Death of Decius Mus in Battle, 1617

center of the picture, the warrior-leader falls dying from his horse, his neck pierced by an enemy's spear. Dead and wounded men in the foreground serve as a grisly base for the bloody action. Having been forewarned in a dream that his troops would falter and retreat, he has thrown himself into the heart of the fray, sacrificing his life in an effort to spur his men. The soldiers, as the story goes, took courage from his example, regrouped themselves and won the day.

45

No one had ever portrayed men and animals in combat in quite the same way as Rubens. Previous artists had made accurate studies of both wild and tame beasts and had pictured them in scenes involving men. Such works were usually designed to show off a knowledge of animal anatomy or were based on historical, Biblical or mythological stories.

Rubens' imagination leaped beyond reality, history and allegory to create a vivid world in which men and beasts are pitted against one another in elemental conflicts. Physical power, courage and excitement characterize his hunting spectacles, a genre that he popularized during the middle of his career.

The bold scene shown here—one of four commissioned by Duke Maximilian of Bavaria for one of his palaces—portrays an unlikely struggle involving a crocodile, a beleaguered hippopotamus, three dogs, trio of horses and five men. Rubens' composition masterfully concentrates all the boiling energy of the picture in the figure of the hippo. The curve of the crocodile's spine leads the viewer's eye upward. There, spread out like a fan across the top of the painting, the horses' long faces, the raised arms of the hunters, the spears and swords, provide strong diagonals that are carefully designed to redirect attention downward into the center of action. In this way Rubens organized the diversity of forms in his picture so that they would hold together, and he heightened the drama by concentrating all the viewer's attention on the life and death animal struggle in the heart of the painting.

47

The Hippopotamus Hunt, c. 1615-1616

In his hunting scenes, Rubens played not only on the viewers' emotional reactions to moments of personal courage—as in the painting shown here—but also on their interest in exotic subjects. Europe was still discovering the rest of the world. Few Europeans had seen Moors, Arabs, desert palm trees, hippos or most of the other African or Indian animals that are so familiar today. When Rubens had an opportunity to see exotic beasts, as he often did in the private menageries of noblemen for whom he worked, he studied and sketched them carefully *(see page 120)*, realizing their potential appeal as subjects for his large animal paintings.

He also was doubtless pleased to demonstrate his erudition by painting animals that were unfamiliar to most of his contemporaries. He usually included several species in one painting—five are shown in the hunt scene on the preceding pages, five are evident here—in a manner that sometimes stretched biological authenticity but that amply satisfied his desire for visual impact.

It is clear from these works that Rubens intended them mainly to entertain. In the painting at right, for example, the central rider being clawed from his horse by a tiger is pictured with remarkable restraint. He is not screaming frantically, or in panic. Rubens' control keeps the work from being gruesome or repellent. As one observer noted, there is a "certain delicious horror here," but Rubens was fully aware of the distinction between good melodrama and macabre sensationalism.

Tigers and Lions Hunt, 1617-1618

Fall of the Damned, 1620

One of Rubens' greatest Baroque masterpieces, a panoramic scene in which masses of naked figures are strung like garlands across the picture surface, imaginatively re-creates that day at the end of eternity when the Bible says the blessed will be raised to Heaven and the damned forever consigned to Hell. Commissioned for a Jesuit church in Neuburg, Germany, it is one of several versions of the torments of the damned that Rubens painted, and it was preceded by many preliminary studies and sketches.

The composition, filled with a great turmoil of bodies and strong contrasts of light and color, is masterfully organized. Silhouetted against a slash of brilliant sky at the top of which St. Michael hurls a thunderbolt and angels guard the way to Heaven, a river of tortured figures streams down diagonally from the upper right center of the picture toward the middle, where a tangle of biting devils *(detail at right)* pulls the fleshy bodies of sinners into the fires of Hell. From there, the composition swoops upward to the right past a Hydra-headed monster who plucks bodies from the air like so many gnats. Splashed with light and set in deep space, the picture is one of the most powerful works of the visual imagination ever created by an artist.

III

A Golden Foundation

In this moving composition, in which the Roman soldier Longinus inflicts Christ's final wound, Rubens contrasts the radiant and tranquil Christ figure—triumphant in death, His suffering over—with the writhing bodies of the two thieves, caught at a peak of physical and emotional torment.

Le Coup de Lance, 1620

When Rubens told the Duke of Mantua's secretary in 1608 that he would return to Italy after visiting his family in Antwerp, he had every intention of keeping his promise. Already one of the best known of the Northern painters in Rome, he had a growing circle of friends and patrons, and he loved Italy at this time perhaps even more than his own country. He thought he would be back within a few months.

Fast as he traveled, Rubens arrived in Antwerp to find that his mother was already dead. All that he could do was to put up over her tomb as a monument to the "best of mothers" the noble altarpiece that he had originally designed for the Chiesa Nuova and that he believed to be the finest picture he had yet painted.

Family events of a happier kind prevented his immediate return to Rome. His brother Philip was to be married in March 1609, and Peter Paul was much occupied as master of ceremonies. Delighted with the occasion, he wrote to a friend in Rome: "We have been so involved in the marriage of my brother that we have been unable to attend to anything but serving the ladies. . . . My brother has been favored by Venus, Cupid, Juno and all the gods: there has fallen to his lot a wife who is beautiful, learned, gracious, wealthy and well born. . . . It was a fortunate hour when he laid aside the scholar's gown and dedicated himself to the service of Cupid. I myself will not dare to follow him, for he has made such a good choice that it seems inimitable. And I should not like to have my bride called ugly if she were inferior to his."

Rubens was apparently having doubts, too, about his intention of returning to Italy. The letter continues: "I have not yet made up my mind whether to remain in my own country or to return forever to Rome. . . . The Archduke and the Most Serene Infanta have had letters written urging me to remain in their service. Their offers are very generous, but I have little desire to become a courtier again. Antwerp and its citizens would satisfy me if I could say farewell to Rome. A peace treaty, or rather, a truce for many years, will without doubt be ratified, and during this period it is believed that our country will flourish again."

The letter reveals the pleasurable indecision that agitated his mind.

Should he settle down, after all, in his own country? There were several arguments in favor of that course. In the first place, as events were to prove, marriage was not so far from his mind as he indicated. And then the offer from the governors of the Spanish Netherlands, the Archduke and the Archduchess (or the Serene Infanta, as Rubens preferred to call her, giving her her Spanish title) was an attractive one.

One factor that made it so was the truce of which Rubens wrote in his letter. A cessation of hostilities for 12 years between the Spanish Netherlands and the United Provinces of the North was proclaimed in April 1609. It was not a final peace; Philip III of Spain had not abandoned the hope of reuniting the Netherlands under the Catholic rule of the Spanish Crown, if necessary by the resumption of war at the end of the 12 years. Still less had the Dutch of the Northern Provinces abandoned their determination to defend the independence for which they had fought. But in the meantime friendly relations were renewed throughout the Netherlands, and for the first time in more than 40 years the noise of war was stilled.

As rulers of the Southern Netherlands, the Archduke Albert and the Archduchess Isabella did all in their power to restore the prosperity of their subjects by encouraging industry, stimulating commerce and generously patronizing the arts. Both were conscientious and hard-working rulers, but the Archduchess was the more remarkable of the two. She had studied the art of government at the side of her father, Philip II, at an age when most girls are studying the art of adornment in a mirror. Well informed on every aspect of European politics, humane and intelligent, she also had sound judgment and strength of character.

It had been her father's wish that she and her husband, who was also her cousin, should found a new dynasty to rule the Netherlands as an independent state in alliance with Spain. But she was over 30 at the time of her marriage and it was apparent within a few years that she would be childless. Perhaps for this reason she gave to the government of the Netherlands something very like maternal devotion.

Rubens painted the royal pair several times during his career *(page 20)*. He depicted the Archduke as a serious and dignified man, for whom he undoubtedly felt sincere respect as well as gratitude—it was, after all, Albert who had given him his first important commission for an altarpiece in Rome. But his strongest feeling of loyalty was toward the Archduchess, for whom his affection and respect deepened with the years. His later portraits of her are drawn with a sympathetic understanding that allows us to read all the qualities and virtues in her striking but by no means conventionally beautiful face.

Besides his allegiance to Albert and Isabella, Rubens felt an obligation, as well as a desire, to assist in the revival of his country. Naturally, he was also aware that there would be much work for artists when time and money were available to restore and beautify the churches and public buildings damaged in the long years of war.

There were several other factors tempting Rubens to remain home. His brother Philip pressed him to stay, and Peter Paul set much store on their close relationship. Furthermore, Rubens was welcomed by many of his old friends among the painters of Antwerp. In June of 1609 he was elected to the distinguished brotherhood of the Romanists, men who had studied in Italy. He was formally accepted into their midst by Jan Brueghel, son of the Pieter Brueghel who had immortalized the peasant life of the Netherlands, and who himself enjoyed European fame for his exquisite still-life paintings of fruit and flowers.

Finally, and perhaps most persuasive of all, Rubens found himself in love. Isabella Brant was the niece of Philip's new wife, and Rubens had seen her a good deal at the festivities during Philip's wedding. She was the daughter of one of Antwerp's most wealthy and cultured citizens, Jan Brant, who throughout his long life was to be a valued friend to Rubens. Isabella and Rubens lived on the same street at the time, and it may be that Philip's wife exploited this proximity and skillfully encouraged Peter Paul's wooing in order to bind him to Antwerp with ties he could not break. At any rate, it did not take Rubens long to set his heart on the charming young Isabella, and to discover that his love was returned.

With all these considerations in his mind, Rubens finally came to a decision in the summer of 1609: he would accept the offer from the court, he would marry Isabella, open a studio and settle down in Antwerp. He wasted no time acting on the decision. By September he was, in the expressive phrase of a biographer, "bound by chains of gold" to the service of the court in Brussels. In literal fact the Archduke and Archduchess sent him their portraits on a gold chain together with notice of his appointment as a court painter at a handsome, tax-exempt salary.

In the years following his appointment, the work that Rubens undertook for the court, such as painting portraits of members of the court circle or decorative works for palaces and chapels, did not interfere with the very large number of commissions he accepted from other patrons both within the Spanish Netherlands and abroad. Furthermore, he even dictated to some extent the terms of his employment. Court painters often were allotted rooms in or near the royal palace in Brussels, but Rubens stipulated that he must live in Antwerp. As he had written to his friend in Rome, he did not want "to become a courtier again."

How Rubens got such consideration is not known; it was no light matter to secure special terms when serving royal masters in the 17th Century. But there is ample evidence that Rubens, all his life, combined graceful manners with remarkable obstinacy in matters relating to his career. An English patron who some years later tried to argue with him about his prices described, with wry humor, how the "cruel courteous painter" had refused to lower the figure. There must have been something of this polite immovability about his attitude to the offers of the Archduke and the Archduchess. Indeed, it may have been the successful handling of his own affairs that prompted the perceptive Archduchess in later years to launch her gifted painter on his extraordinary career as an international diplomat.

A few weeks after his court appointment, Rubens married Isabella. At 18, she was not much more than half her husband's age, but she was to prove a perfect wife, "free of moodiness and of the usual weak-

Anthony van Dyck, Rubens' most celebrated assistant and collaborator, became the leading portraitist of his era. He made the self-portrait above, and the studies of other Rubens associates on these pages, for *Iconographia*, his collection of 100 etchings of famous men and women of his time. Jan Brueghel, the flower painter and landscapist, is shown below.

nesses of women, all goodness, all sincerity," as Rubens was later to describe her. Though attractive, she was not beautiful, nor was she the physical type that Rubens most admired. Already in some of his pictures—notably in the portrayal of St. Domitilla in his altarpiece for the Chiesa Nuova in Rome—he had shown his predilection for women of large proportions, dazzling skin and golden hair; Isabella, by contrast, was dark, with a small, pointed face and amusingly tilted eyebrows over lively, observant eyes. But there is no doubt of his devotion to her during the 17 years of their union.

Rubens celebrated his marriage by painting a double portrait of rare enchantment *(page 17)*. He and Isabella sit hand in hand in a bower of honeysuckle. His pose is artfully casual, with one silk-stockinged leg crossed over the other; she has settled down on a stool beside him, with her elegant skirts outspread. Their joined hands are the center of the composition. Both look out of the picture toward the spectator with happy confidence. They are two healthy, attractive, superlatively well-dressed young people, well pleased with life and with each other.

It is a delightful picture, having little in common with the formal representations of husbands and wives that had hitherto been the rule. Rubens had never painted anything quite like it before and was never to paint anything quite like it again.

While he was in Italy Rubens had painted many portraits. Genoese patrician families in particular had been his constant patrons. At the end of the 16th Century the prevailing style in European portrait painting had laid strong emphasis on the insignia of wealth and rank, making much of the jewels, brocades and huge ruffs that were then in vogue. This emphasis had dehumanized the portrait, just as the wiry stiffness of the fashionable clothes had dehumanized the body. Rubens frankly loved the glitter of gems, the texture of velvet and brocade, but his genius breathed life into his pictures by making the magnificent clothes an expression of personality as well as rank. Under his brush the character of the subject dominated even the large and formal portraits that he executed within the convention of the Italian grand manner.

But his wedding portrait, which reflects a resurgent love for his country as well as the pride and pleasure he took in his charming young wife, represented a return to the direct and highly finished manner that was traditional in the Netherlands. The quaint, slightly humorous posing of the figures among honeysuckle and flowers, symbols of love and fidelity, the jewel-like brightness of the coloring and the meticulous treatment of every detail of their clothes recall the minuscule precision of such early Flemish painters as Hans Memling and Jan van Eyck. It is, in fact, a triumphantly Flemish picture.

A period of hope and revival had dawned in Antwerp with the truce of 1609, but time was to show that any hope for a long-term economic revival was ill founded. During the years of war and division, Amsterdam had risen to power and Antwerp could no longer compete on equal terms. Not until the industrial and commercial changes of the 19th Century would Antwerp again become a major center of European trade.

But culturally and esthetically Antwerp came to stand high among

European cities during the years of truce and for some time afterward—an achievement in which Rubens himself was very much involved. The wide streets, the marketplaces, the handsome public buildings and the great harbor may have seemed too large for the reduced number of citizens and the volume of trade, but the intellectual life of the city was vigorous and exciting.

The strongest current of inspiration came from the Church. A renewal of Catholic faith, inspired by the activities of the reformed religious orders and the preaching of the Jesuits, stimulated the restoration of damaged churches and the building of new ones and filled the churches with devout worshipers. Altarpieces, statues, stained-glass windows and tapestry hangings were commissioned in great numbers. But the building and beautifying were not confined to churches. Public buildings too were enlarged and enriched, while private citizens improved their houses partly for their own comfort and dignity, and partly out of a sense of civic pride.

It was, as Rubens had foreseen, a fortunate time for an artist to be in Antwerp. During the blessed years of peace between 1609 and 1621 Rubens painted altarpieces for the Antwerp cathedral and for the most important of the city's churches, new and old, as well as for the principal churches of nearby Malines and Ghent.

Many other artists of talent, and a few of genius, also contributed to the fame of the Antwerp school at this time. Besides Jan Brueghel, nine years older than Rubens, there was Frans Snyders, a masterly painter of animals. Somewhat younger was Jacob Jordaens who, like Rubens, had studied under Adam van Noort, and who painted solid, succulent pictures of boisterous Flemish life and of mythological scenes filled with ample nudes. And there was young Anthony van Dyck, with his fluent, lyrical touch, who began his brilliant career working at Rubens' side.

Generally, Rubens fitted well into this artistic community, as was evidenced by his warm welcome among the Romanists. Although his wide scope, his speed of working, richness of imagination and technical skill put him rapidly ahead of all competitors, Rubens was both generous and tactful. He was respectful to his elders and remained on excellent terms with his last teacher, Otto van Veen, and even with his earlier master, Adam van Noort, who had a reputation for being captious and difficult. As for Jan Brueghel, Rubens seems to have regarded him somewhat as an elder brother. They collaborated on a number of pictures, with Rubens painting the figures and Brueghel the decorative flowers and fruit—a partnership in which it would seem that Brueghel, rather than Rubens, was the senior partner. In spite of the heavy pressure of his own work, Rubens even served for several years as an unofficial secretary to Brueghel for his Italian correspondence. Brueghel had valuable connections in Italy but could not match the elegant ease with which Rubens spoke and wrote the language.

Rubens was on equally good terms with Frans Snyders, whose work he admired, though he objected—with justified vanity—when a patron took some of his own animal paintings for the work of Snyders. No one, he said, could depict *dead* animals better than his friend Snyders, but for live animals, he was himself the better painter.

Van Dyck included his fellow painters Frans Snyders *(above)* and Jacob Jordaens *(below)* among the princes, scholars and artists whom he honored in his *Iconographia*. Although van Dyck etched only about 18 of the 100 plates, the rest were completed by master engravers from models supplied by him and they invariably bear the mark of his sensitive, lively and elegant style.

Still, Rubens could not have been popular with everyone. Some jealousy was inevitable, and it is surprising there was not more of it. Until Rubens' return from Rome, his contemporary Abraham Janssens, who had come back from Italy a few years earlier, regarded himself as the best painter of his generation in Antwerp. The two artists came into immediate competition when both received commissions for the decoration of the town hall. Janssens produced a handsome allegorical group in the manner of Veronese, showing Antwerp as a beautiful nymph, with a river god representing the Scheldt. Rubens painted an *Adoration of the Kings* for the same room.

This was the first of many versions of the Adoration that Rubens was to paint in Flanders. It is an immense, crowded picture, lit by flaring torches that illuminate the kings in glowing red and gold robes and the graceful Virgin supporting the Infant on His humble bed of straw. The painting was greatly enlarged and enriched by Rubens at a later date; but even in its original state it must have attracted far more attention than the conventional work of Janssens that hung nearby. Possibly it was this invidious juxtaposition that caused Janssens to issue a sneering challenge to his rival. He suggested that if each of them were to paint a picture of a given subject, and submit the results to a dispassionate judge who did not know which picture was which, his own would doubtless be preferred. Rubens evaded the challenge, which he felt was likely to prove more damaging to Janssens than to himself. Why compete? he asked his fellow artist; neither of them could do better than their best.

Soon after this incident, Rubens was commissioned to paint his first altarpiece in Antwerp, for the altar of the Gothic church of St. Walburga. (The altarpiece is now in the cathedral of Antwerp.) He chose a subject that he had first attempted eight years earlier in Rome, the *Elevation of the Cross (page 70)*, and he made of it a dramatic and powerful composition. The monumental groups of spectators, soldiers and horses on two side panels form a dark, restless setting for the central scene showing Christ on the Cross and the straining bodies of the executioners. The Savior's body has a classical nobility, with upraised arms and lifted head expressive of both heroism and sacrifice, and the emphasis is on the victory rather than the horror of the Cross.

So that the altarpiece should make its effect down the long perspective of a Gothic church, Rubens used strong contrasts of light and shade, which owe something to the work of Tintoretto that he had studied in Venice, and something also to Caravaggio. In this picture, as in most of the others he painted at this time, the color was still warmly Venetian, a harmony of reds and browns in golden light without a trace of the cool, watery reflections of the Netherlands. Belatedly, since his return home, he had fallen under the influence of Caravaggio, adopting his manner of painting bold, life-sized figures and showing them just from the waist up, singly or in groups.

The religious revival had led to a great increase in manuals of devotion and to a widespread demand for pictures of Christ crucified. The figure of the dying Savior, symbol of redemption, was needed not only for churches but also for the chapels of great houses and for the private devotions of the faithful. The tragic vision of the suffering Man-God, rather than the gentler image of the Madonna and Child, was the foundation of Counter Reformation worship. The subject could not possibly be treated differently every time it was painted, and in the 17th Century two dominating versions of Christ were widely imitated.

One came from Guido Reni, the other from Rubens. Guido, a Bolognese painter, was almost exactly the same age as Rubens and had been in Rome at the same time. There is no evidence to suggest any contact between them, although both in their different ways responded to the same influences—Raphael, Correggio, Caravaggio, Carracci, as well as the masters of antiquity. Guido's conception of the Crucifixion is tender and unheroic. Christ hangs on the Cross with arms outstretched and hands open, almost in an attitude of blessing. There is no evidence of struggle in the submissive body, luminous against a murky sky.

On the other hand, the Crucifixion as Rubens interpreted it is neither gentle nor consoling. The emphasis is on triumph through suffering, and on the agonizing death of the human flesh. The Cross is austerely narrow and the arms of Christ, instead of being outspread, are raised almost straight above His head; the muscles of the body are tense and strained, the fingers clenched and the head twisted in the last extremity of pain. The worshipers for whom such a picture was intended were to be left in no doubt as to the magnitude of the sacrifice that had been made for them. And yet the upward-straining body and the uplifted arms give to the figure an aspect of heroic triumph.

Rubens appears to have created this figure soon after his return from Italy. He used it with variations several times *(pages 52, 136)*; his assistants copied it; Anthony van Dyck adapted it. It can be seen, in one form or another, in many picture galleries and churches, and it has been dispersed by means of cheap reproduction over the whole Catholic world. In the process it has therefore lost some of its impact. But to look at a good version of it, from the hand of Rubens himself, can still be a deeply moving experience; and it tells much about the faith and discipline that were the hard core of his achievement.

Faith and discipline are not, perhaps, the words that first suggest themselves as being appropriate to Rubens, who is more often thought of as the sumptuous interpreter of pagan and mythological subjects. But it was characteristic of post-Renaissance European art that painters were often called upon to celebrate the Christian faith in ecclesiastical buildings and the sensuality and poetry of Classical mythology in secular ones. There was therefore nothing unusual in a painter who turned with ease from one to the other.

The art of Rubens was extraordinary in the clarity with which it reflected this attitude of Counter Reformation humanists—men like Justus Lipsius and Rubens' own brother Philip. They admired the ancients for the beauty of their writing and the fecundity of their ideas, but also saw in pagan mythology a kind of indirect tribute to the power of the Christians' one God, because these beautiful false imaginings had in the end made way for the triumph of Christ.

Thus, when Rubens painted a mythological or Classical subject, he glorified the vigor of universal creation and expressed his own joy in the beauty of the world. But when he painted a religious subject, he was expressing his deepest convictions. Every day of his life, as his nephew Philip later recorded, he heard Mass at an early hour before he started work; this was no mere conventional observance but was the guiding inspiration of his daily life.

In the years following his return from Italy, Rubens painted a great many mythological pictures in which he effectively combined his mastery of Venetian color and his study of early Roman art. A graceful group of Venus, Ceres, Bacchus and Cupid has the flowing beauty of a frieze. A gorgeously colored *Juno and Argus*, with its striking blend of vivid blue, carmine, green and amber recalls the bold brilliance of a Veronese. Most pleasing of all, perhaps, is the *Shivering Venus*, in which the goddess crouches in the cold with golden hair forlornly drooping, protecting a plump Cupid under her scanty veil. This Venus is a version of a Greco-Roman statue Rubens had drawn some years earlier in Italy.

A more powerful mythological picture is Rubens' terrifying *Prometheus Bound (page 72)*. According to Classical legend, Prometheus stole the secret of fire from the gods and gave it to man. To punish him for this misdemeanor, Zeus bound him to a rock where he was to be tortured for all time by a devouring eagle. In painting his larger-than-life-sized picture, Rubens created a powerful effect by showing Prometheus with massive foreshortened limbs and by having the eagle's wings span the captive giant in a great predatory arc. Snyders, who was working in Rubens' studio at the time, actually painted the eagle, but the conception and design belonged to Rubens. The picture, showing as it does the Titan with nothing to sustain him but physical strength and angry pride, is the embodiment of unredeemed torment.

Early in 1611 Rubens received from Rome the sad news of his friend Adam Elsheimer's death. The unfortunate, debt-ridden Elsheimer had been harried by creditors until anxieties hampered his inspiration and undermined his health. He left a widow and son in dire poverty. The practical Rubens at once offered to help dispose of Elsheimer's pictures to raise money for the family, and he inquired particularly after a small *Flight into Egypt*, which he greatly admired. A few years later, he himself painted a *Flight into Egypt*. It is a poetic pilgrimage by moonlight; the Virgin holds her sleeping Child in the fold of her mantle and an angel leads the patient ass while Joseph trudges behind. The nocturnal lighting, the air of hushed mystery, the relation of the human group to the darkened landscape were all reminiscent of Elsheimer, as though the picture had been painted as a tribute to his memory.

A more personal sorrow struck Rubens in August 1611 when Philip died suddenly and unexpectedly at the age of 38. His widow gave birth to a son 15 days later. The child, called Philip, was brought up by Peter Paul and Isabella. But Rubens felt the loss of his elder brother deeply. They had been very close since their boyhood in Cologne, and Peter Paul also had looked up to Philip as a scholar who had become one of the foremost Classicists of the age. Peter Paul painted the picture *The Four Philosophers (page 24)* partly as a memorial to his brother. The scholar Justus

A title page for a prayer book was among many illustrations that Rubens provided for his friend Balthasar Moretus, head of the Plantin press. Atop a simple architectural form—left blank to receive the book's title —he placed an allegorical figure representing Ecclesia, the Church. At left is St. Paul with his emblem, a sword; on the right is St. Peter holding his traditional symbol, a key; at the bottom, flanking the coat of arms of Pope Paul V, are the harp and crowned turban of the Psalmist David.

Lipsius is shown seated below a bust of Seneca; on either side of him are his two best pupils, Jan Woverius and Philip Rubens, while in the background, as a spectator rather than as a participant, stands Peter Paul.

At the time of his premature death, Philip had been at work on an edition of the sermons of the Fifth Century bishop and preacher, St. Asterius. His family and friends published it posthumously as a memorial to him. Balthasar Moretus, the old schoolfriend of the Rubens brothers, was now the director of the Plantin press. He printed the book, which is prefaced by an account of Philip's life written by Isabella's father, Jan Brant, and has for a title page a portrait engraved from a drawing by Peter Paul.

The first time Rubens and Moretus had collaborated on the production of a book was with the publication in 1608 of Philip's work on Roman customs. Now, Rubens' connection with the Plantin-Moretus press became even closer. He provided illustrations for a beautiful edition of the Catholic missal which came out in 1613 and for an edition of the breviary in the following year.

For the next 25 years Rubens continued to supply Moretus with illustrations for title pages for all manner of books, from the Lipsius edition of the philosophical writings of Seneca to a treatise on optics. His method was simple and cost him a minimum of time. Moretus would let him know, several months in advance, what illustrations were required. He was then able to jot down ideas at his leisure and work them up, in an idle moment, into drawings suitable for engraving.

This capacity for using every instant of available time was the secret of Rubens' gigantic output. The secret of his financial success was the fairness of his prices; he charged for his work as much as he thought it was worth, but never more. He could easily have exacted a high price for his spare-time jottings, but he would not have thought it right to do so.

Rubens was interested in engraving for another reason besides illustrating Moretus' books. In those days, and, indeed, until the advent of photography, art lovers had to depend on an erratic supply of painted copies and engravings for their knowledge of works of art. Rubens perceived, with his usual level-headedness, that a painter who organized the engravings of his own pictures, instead of leaving the matter to chance, would be able to make his work very widely known.

Rubens himself did not do any engraving, but he knew enough about the art to adapt his style of drawing to it. He was particular about the quality of the engraving work, and liked to supervise it himself. For several years after his return to Antwerp, he tried various engravers and finally settled on one whose technique satisfied him. This was the talented and sensitive Lucas Vorsterman, who developed an astonishing skill in rendering subtle gradations of light and shade. Within a few years, owing to Rubens' typically deft blend of artistic virtuosity and business acumen, engravings of his paintings were selling in great numbers, and at considerable profit to him, in the United Provinces and France as well as in the Spanish Netherlands; by the mid-1620s he also had a market in England, Germany and Italy.

At the time of his marriage, Rubens did not own a house and he lived initially with his father-in-law. But in two years his first child, Clara Serena, was born, and his family required more room. Furthermore, as the volume of his work increased, so did his need for space—partly for his own painting, and partly to accommodate the pupils who flocked to work in his studio. As he wrote to a friend in Brussels, "It is impossible for me to accept the young man whom you recommend. From all sides applications reach me. Some young men remain here for several years with other masters, awaiting a vacancy in my studio. . . . I can tell you truly, without any exaggeration, that I have had to refuse over one hundred, even some of my own relatives or my wife's, and not without causing great displeasure among many of my best friends."

So Rubens bought a house. It was a comfortable gabled mansion of brick and stone that had been standing for about 90 years—and that is still standing, though extensively reconstructed *(pages 25, 26, 27 and 94, 95)*. It had a large courtyard, a garden and some adjoining land. He purchased the house with the intention of extending it, and for several years after he moved in, the building operations went on. Though the original dwelling had handsome carved chimney pieces and tiled floors, it was otherwise unpretentious, and Rubens kept it that way. But on the garden side he added a well-proportioned hall in which he set out the antique busts and statues that he had collected in his Italian journey or had bought since his return. On the open land adjoining the house he built a spacious studio on two levels, an upper floor for his pupils and assistants, the lower and larger hall for himself. The studio building was of stone, in the Italian manner, with pediments over the windows and the outer walls richly decorated with carvings and busts; it was linked to the house by graceful columns. The open space enclosed by house and studio was divided from the garden and converted into a courtyard by a stone screen, surmounted by statues and pierced by three arched doorways through which the formal garden and a small Classical pavilion could be seen.

Soon after they were established in the new house, the Rubenses took in their infant nephew, Philip; within a few years two sons, Albert and Nicolas, were born to them to complete the family circle.

As Rubens' domestic affairs prospered, so did his artistic reputation. But he experienced an occasional setback. One such reversal involved a large altarpiece commissioned for St. Bavon, the principal church of Ghent. Rubens designed a splendid triptych, and from a small version, or *modello,* that still exists one can imagine how magnificent the completed altarpiece would have been. But at the critical moment a new bishop was appointed in Ghent. The bishop, as Rubens complained to the Archduke, "without even once looking at my designs . . . has allowed himself to be persuaded to erect a most preposterous high altar without a picture of any sort." The dispute dragged on for some years and ended in a compromise, with Rubens producing a single and much less ambitious painting than the large triptych that had at first been planned.

In contrast to this disappointment was the transcendent success of an altarpiece that he painted between 1611 and 1614 for the cathedral at Antwerp. It was commissioned by the Arquebusiers, one of the many quasi-military brotherhoods in the Netherlands at that time, for a side chapel reserved for their worship in the cathedral. They asked Rubens for a triptych with four pictures in all—a central panel with two hinged wings painted on both sides—and stipulated that their patron, St. Christopher, who according to Christian legend had borne Christ across a river, should appear somewhere in the composition. They offered Rubens the very considerable price of 2,400 florins. (Just how good a price this was is indicated by the fact that it was equivalent to about one third of the price of Rubens' house, which was considered to be a very expensive property.)

Rubens depicted St. Christopher as a Herculean giant, with a small Christ Child perched on his shoulder. This picture covered the reverse of the side panels, and was visible only when the wings of the triptych were closed. The principal picture was the *Deposition from the Cross;* on the left was the *Visitation,* and on the right, the *Presentation in the Temple.*

The *Visitation* and the *Presentation* are compositions of singular grace, painted in the warm colors that are still reminiscent of Venice. But the central *Deposition (page 71)* marks an emancipation from Italian influence and the evolution of a lighter range of color that is more typical of Northern painting. In the dead body, the winding sheet and the women's figures, shimmering whites and grays, pale amber and blue-green contrast with the more traditional reds and browns of the male figures.

But, important though they are, the beauty of the color and rhythmic subtlety of the composition are not what first strike the beholder. The eye is immediately riveted by the figure of the dead Christ. "One of the finest figures that ever was invented," wrote Sir Joshua Reynolds when he stood in wonder before it more than a hundred years later. "The hanging of the head on His shoulder, and the falling of the body on one side, give such an appearance of the heaviness of death that nothing can exceed it." The "heaviness of death" is indeed expressed, yet there is nothing heavy about the picture. With a breathtaking virtuosity, Rubens has caught the very instant after the body has been released from the Cross and before it falls with all its weight against the stalwart arms of St. John, who stands braced to receive it. A workman slightly supports Christ's left arm, while on His right the venerable Nicodemus holds a part of the winding sheet and steadies the body. The kneeling Magdalen reaches up to support the feet. But no one as yet is taking the weight; it is the critical moment, the split second of time before the inert Christ subsides into the outstretched arms.

In 1682, 42 years after Rubens' death, this engraving of his Antwerp house was made, showing his dwelling, at left, connected by a colonnade to his studio. The house was almost completely rebuilt during the 18th Century, and when the city of Antwerp bought the place in 1937 to establish it as a museum, this picture was one of the few visual guides the architects could use in their work of restoration *(pages 24-25).*

The *Deposition* was a challenge to painters because it demanded extreme technical skill in drawing, together with the power to arouse emotion in the beholder. Rubens had studied some of the most famous interpretations of the theme in Italy and his picture reveals the influence of versions by Ludovico Cigoli and Daniele da Volterra, a favorite disciple of Michelangelo. But Rubens' *Deposition*—the greatest he had yet painted and one of the greatest he was ever to paint—was both more realistic and more deeply felt than those from which he drew his inspiration. To his contemporaries it was much more than a triumph of color, form and design: it spoke to them with compelling eloquence of the central theme of their faith. Within a few years the fame of it had spread throughout Western Europe. It was this picture that established Rubens as the foremost religious painter of his time, and the first to express the full emotional intensity of the Baroque.

A Vigorous Faith

In 1540, Ignatius of Loyola *(right)*, a Spanish soldier-cleric, founded the Society of Jesus, dedicated to the revitalization of Roman Catholicism. The order flourished, and by 1610 it was the dominant religious force of the Counter Reformation. Sophisticated and scholarly, the Jesuits were intensely interested in the intellectual and artistic traditions of both the Christian and the Classical, or pagan, past. To promulgate their beliefs, and to encourage a greater participation among worshipers, Jesuit leaders stimulated activity in all the arts: music, drama, architecture, sculpture and painting. In seeking more personal and exciting expressions of the religious spirit, they commissioned art in which the austerity and impersonality of earlier styles were gradually replaced by passion, energy and an often blatantly theatrical emotionality. The Baroque style that Rubens and other artists working for the order evolved blended religious and secular forms, and perfectly suited the Jesuits' dedication to proclaiming the glory of God.

Rubens' own talents, shaped by his exposure to Italian art, as well as by his own energetic and far-ranging mind, combined with his deep devotion to Catholicism to make him a favorite artist of the Jesuits. Many of his finest works were painted for them, and their patronage undoubtedly influenced the character of much of his religious art for other orders, for noble patrons, and—in the case of at least one work, his own tomb painting—for himself.

In a magnificent cathedral, St. Ignatius Loyola dramatically implores God to exorcise demons from the sick and lame. The work was commissioned by the Jesuits as an altarpiece for their first Antwerp church, later named in honor of St. Charles Borromeo. It was placed in the church on the occasion of Ignatius' canonization in 1622.

The Miracles of
St. Ignatius Loyola, 1620

One of Rubens' most important religious projects—and his largest early commission—was to provide the Jesuits with three altarpieces and 39 ceiling paintings for St. Charles Borromeo in Antwerp *(opposite page)*. In addition to these canvases, Rubens designed some of the decorations for the church façade, and suggested various architectural details for the interior. An example of his participation is the sketch shown at left, for the stone relief that appears above the arch of the main portal of the church.

Disaster struck the church in 1718. A lightning bolt hit the tower and caused a fire that destroyed much of the interior. The three enormous altarpieces were rescued, but every one of Rubens' ceiling paintings was lost. Fortunately, the artist's contract with the Jesuits had required him to submit sample sketches in oils for each proposed painting, and many of these still exist. One *(below)* portrays a Fourth Century saint striking a figure symbolizing Heresy with his bishop's crozier. The swirling excitement of this study provides a hint of how the richness of Rubens' brilliant finished works must have illuminated the church interior.

Cartouche Supported by Cherubs, c. 1617-1620

St. Gregory Nazianzus, 1620

The Church of St. Charles Borromeo, Antwerp

D · O · M
OSTIUM
MONUMENTI
FAMILIÆ RUBENIANÆ

Madonna with Saints, c. 1636-1640

Great religious painters are not necessarily devout believers. Rubens, however, was a pious man who accepted and executed religious commissions with enthusiasm. One of his most stunning works is the picture above, which he ordered placed above his tomb, in a chapel that he asked his wife to have built in his memory.

Considerable uncertainty surrounds the work. Rubens probably painted it for himself very late in his career, although no exact date is known. Tradition has it that the figures of the Madonna and Mary Magdalen represent the artist's wives, that the bearded St. Jerome in the foreground is Rubens' father and that St. George, at the left, is a self-portrait. Whatever its background, the painting is a fitting monument to its maker. It stands in the Rubens family chapel in the Church of St. Jacques in Antwerp *(left)*, set into an ornate marble tabernacle that is believed to have been carved by Lucas Fayd'herbe, a young sculptor whom Rubens had befriended.

Elevation of the Cross, c. 1610-1611

The two large triptychs shown on these pages, whose 15-foot-high central panels are reproduced above, provide an unusual opportunity to examine the development of Rubens' artistry. The *Elevation of the Cross (above)* is an early attempt to come to grips with the dramatic Baroque style; its main compositional line, running from the lower right foreground to the upper left background, creates the illusion of deep

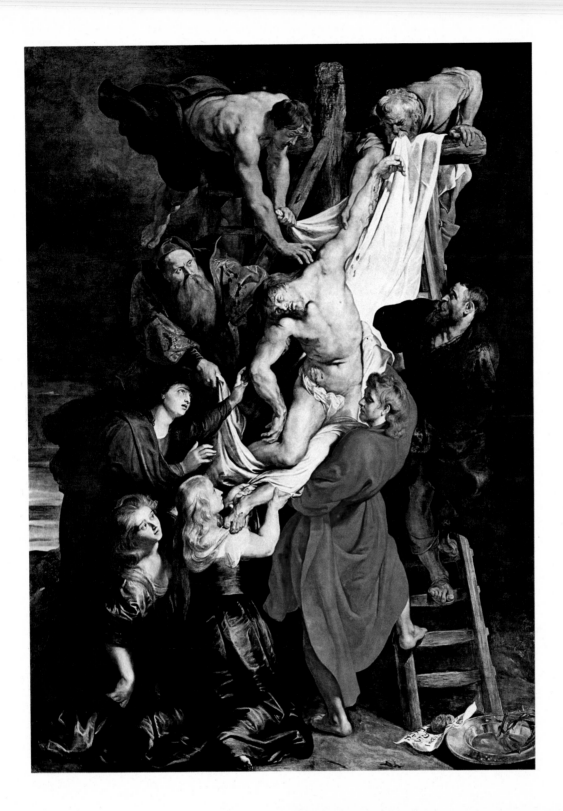

space and movement; straining bodies, an agitated dog and blustery trees add visual excitement. In the Deposition scene, on the other hand, a more mature Baroque style is evident. The picture has a greater unity and organization: it is composed in powerful, sweeping curves that lead the viewer's eye into the center, where tension is focused in the figure of Christ, pitifully slumping into the arms of His followers.

Descent from the Cross, c. 1611-1614

IV

"Prince of Painters"

The spirit of the Catholic Counter Reformation was essentially Puritan. In the superficial sense there was little resemblance—and no sympathy—between 17th Century Roman Catholics and the Puritans of Holland or of Old or New England: Puritans rejected the outward shows of ritual and of church ornaments; Catholics on the other hand heaped adornments on their churches and chapels and enhanced their worship with music and ceremony. But at the core their religious feelings during this epoch were closer than they knew. The devout Roman Catholic, like the devout Puritan, looked upon life as a spiritual pilgrimage, a process of proving himself fit for salvation by subordinating his self-indulgent desires to the will of God and the service of his fellow men. Both Catholic and Puritan believed in the duty of spiritual struggle and honest work.

When his poor friend Adam Elsheimer died, Rubens wrote of him: "I pray that God will forgive Signor Adam his sin of sloth, by which he has deprived the world of the most beautiful things . . . and finally . . . reduced himself to despair." In Rubens' view, the waste of Elsheimer's talent had been not only a cause of material loss but also a sin. Such an opinion could easily have come from a contemporary Puritan.

Rubens' art, however, could not have come from a Puritan. Strict Protestants of the time suspected all—or nearly all—material aids to prayer, viewing ritual, ornaments and pictures as idolatrous interventions between man and God. The Roman Catholic, on the other hand, believed that works of art were themselves manifestations of the goodness of God and could inspire and help the worshiper. Rubens was therefore using the great talents that had been bestowed on him to increase the faith of other believers.

Naturally his art was also his business. The pictures he painted for churches were not given to the churches by him, but by patrons who paid Rubens for his work. There was nothing in Christian morality, Catholic or Protestant, against earning one's living honestly. Rubens' fees were no higher than his reputation warranted; he always gave of his best and was scrupulously conscientious in fulfilling his contracts. With a very few exceptions (like the disappointing affair of the altarpiece for the Cathedral

Although the exact contributions of assistants to some Rubens paintings are unknown, the artist did not hesitate to identify his collaborator on this work. In a letter offering to trade the painting and others for a valuable collection of antique statues, Rubens listed it thus: "Five hundred florins; a Prometheus bound on Mount Caucasus; with an Eagle which pecks his liver. Original by my hand, and the Eagle done by Snyders. Nine feet high by eight feet wide."

Peter Paul Rubens and Frans Snyders: *Prometheus Bound*; 1611-1612

73

of St. Bavon), his relations with the clergy and with his patrons were happy and harmonious.

In 1620 Rubens' friend Nicolas Rockox, the burgomaster of Antwerp, whose portrait he had painted a few years earlier, commissioned him to paint a Crucifixion for the Franciscan Church of the Récollets. This now-famous picture is generally called *Le Coup de Lance (page 52)*, from the action of the Roman soldier who is shown piercing the side of Christ. The little group of Christ's mourners is jostled by soldiers and horses in the narrow spaces between the three stark uprights of the crosses at Calvary. The coarseness and callousness of a public execution is contrasted with the silent grief of the standing Virgin and St. John, and with the compassion of the kneeling Magdalen, who puts out her hands in a helpless gesture of protection as the soldier raises his lance.

At about the same time, Rubens painted one of his most poignant religious pictures, also for the Church of the Récollets. It was the *Last Communion of St. Francis of Assisi*, a painting in which he expressed with a wonderful understanding the self-abandonment of spiritual love. St. Francis, emaciated by fasting, is surrounded and supported by a group of monks; his figure, luminous in its naked pallor, shines out against their dark robes as he leans forward toward the priest and lifts his eyes for the last time to gaze with ecstasy at the Host.

Rubens put all his own faith as well as his painter's skill into this representation of a human soul at the very moment of liberation from the flesh. Esthetic appreciation and religious feeling are here very closely bound up with each other, and if we are to get the full impact of this picture, we must put ourselves in the frame of mind of a different age, in which the existence of the spiritual world was unquestioningly accepted and to which heaven was a physical, though unseen, reality. The earthly realism in Rubens' religious paintings is disturbing, and not the less so because the material solidity of the events on the physical plane is often contrasted—as it is in the *St. Francis*—with a burst of celestial glory and fanciful flights of cherubim in the upper part of the picture. Many of us today "get the message" more easily from a painter like El Greco, whose saints have bodies as incandescent as their spirits.

But Rubens, though he made his figures solid and lifelike, has distilled that glowing spirituality in the face of the dying St. Francis; a face painted with a depth of understanding and humanity equal to that of Rembrandt. This gift for embodying an exalted spiritual state was, indeed, a principal reason for Rubens' fame among his contemporaries.

Of course, Rubens painted many happier religious subjects. His own contented domestic life was mirrored in numerous inventive and charming pictures of the Holy Family. He drew the faces of his sons, Albert and Nicolas, with loving care, and sketched and brought into his paintings the innumerable gestures and attitudes of the young—shy, graceful, comic or adventurous. These studies infused with life his tumbling flights of cherubs and gave a pleasing domestic realism to his pictures of the Holy Family. The presence of two little boys on Rubens' own hearth may have been one reason for his frequent representations of the Madonna and Child with St. Elizabeth and the infant St. John—a traditional theme

74

that he painted with emphasis on the looks and gestures of the two children playing together. He often showed the Holy Family in the open air, and in a bright, clear range of colors. He sometimes included a docile lamb whose curly pelt St. John caresses; in one picture there is a bright blue-and-yellow parrot as a quizzical spectator.

Rubens' most exciting opportunity of these years came from the Jesuits—nothing less than the commission to decorate the vast new church they were building in Antwerp in honor of their founder, Ignatius of Loyola. Rubens was to provide a whole scheme of decoration—39 ceiling paintings. He had already painted two altarpieces showing the two chief Jesuit saints, Ignatius Loyola (*page 65*) and Francis Xavier; later he added a third altarpiece, showing the Assumption. There was need for haste, as the ceiling decorations had to be finished in time for the ceremonies that were to mark the canonization of the two saints in 1622. So Rubens contracted only to design the ceiling paintings himself; they would be completed by his assistants, subject to his own finishing touches.

The huge task was finished in time, and for nearly a century afterward the Jesuit church was one of the principal glories of Antwerp. Then, in 1718, it was gutted by a disastrous fire. The altarpieces were rescued, but the ceiling paintings perished. Later, the church was rededicated to St. Charles Borromeo, by which name it is known today (*page 66*).

Fear of witchcraft was widespread during Rubens' lifetime, and hundreds of books were printed warning of witches' ways. These woodcuts from *Compendium Maleficarum*, a popular collection of evil deeds published in Italy in 1608, show a witches' sabbath (*above*) at which the devil receives homage from his minions, and a village (*below*) supposedly set afire by black magic.

R ubens' sketches for the lost works have survived (*page 67*). Precious as works of art, they are also valuable as evidence of his methods. These swift, masterly outlines show his capacity for creating a picture so completely in his mind's eye that he could set it down in a few brushstrokes with no preliminary drawing. An English connoisseur, Sir William Sanderson, who had evidently watched him at work, once set down his impressions: "Rubens would, with his arms across, sit musing upon his work for some time; and in an instant in the liveliness of spirit, with a nimble hand would force out his overcharged brain into descriptions. . . . The Commotions of the mind are not to be cooled by slow performance."

The archaic English is a vivid footnote to the sketches of Rubens. We can almost see him as Sanderson describes him, thinking with folded arms for a while, then with swift, assured brushstrokes transferring his thoughts to the canvas. The renderings thus executed are small in size but not in quality. There is the style and sweep of the grand manner, often in an area of less than two square feet.

Sketches such as these were the basis of the larger pictures that were worked up by Rubens' assistants, as he had contracted with the Jesuits. This group effort was a method frequently used in studios of the 16th and 17th Centuries, and under pressure of his growing popularity Rubens for a time organized his own studio in this way.

The assistants on whom painters of standing relied under such a system were not, in the ordinary sense, pupils. Pupils prepared the canvases and panels and did other necessary preliminary work, but they would not— at least until they were far advanced in their training—be entrusted with painting from the master's designs. Rubens sought assistance in the actual work of painting from more experienced painters—young artists who had already been accepted as masters by the Guild of St. Luke but who wished to have the further educational experience of working in the studio of a leading artist. Rubens himself had followed this course when he stayed in the studio of his teacher Otto van Veen for at least two years after he had completed his own training.

By far the most famous of Rubens' assistants was the handsome, volatile, fabulously gifted Anthony van Dyck, who became a master in the Guild at the early age of 19. He was 22 years younger than Rubens and was on terms of almost filial friendship with him and his wife. He may even have lived with them briefly; at any rate, he painted for Rubens a lively and sensitive portrait of Isabella. Rubens admired van Dyck's work greatly, and the association between the two painters was so close over a two- or three-year period early in van Dyck's career that there is some confusion today over who painted what during that time.

Van Dyck's gifts were almost as varied as those of Rubens. He had a sharp eye for detail and an exquisite sense of color. Judging from his sketches, he had a great sensibility to landscape, which he expressed in a number of pen-and-ink, chalk, and watercolor drawings. His paintings of religious or mythological subjects show originality of design and a tenderly lyrical imagination.

His greatest distinction was in painting portraits, and over the years he produced hundreds of them. They are full of psychological insight, particularly when he liked the sitter, as in his rendering of his friend the painter Frans Snyders. This and later works, such as the portraits of Charles I of England *(page 85)* and of the Duke of Richmond *(page 86)*, are notable examples of his achievement at its best.

Despite their friendship, Rubens and van Dyck were temperamentally very different and the close similarities in their work did not last long. Linked to the younger man's brilliant talent was a self-centered, extravagant nature, at once too easily flattered and too soon discouraged. He was ambitious and could work hard when he chose but, restless and excitable, he lacked the staying power and judgment that distinguished Rubens, even in his younger days.

The contrast in temperament between Rubens and van Dyck and the effect it had on their work is vividly illustrated by a comparison between the picture by Rubens of *St. Ambrose and the Emperor Theodosius,* and the copy of it by van Dyck. In 390 A.D., St. Ambrose, Bishop of Milan, refused to allow the Roman Emperor to enter Milan Cathedral until he had done penance for an atrocious massacre of the Thessalonians during a campaign in Greece. The painting shows the confrontation between the two men. In the Rubens version of this subject the saint dominates the scene; in his gold-brocaded vestments he is at one and the same time a venerable human personality and a symbol of the moral law. The burly, bearded Emperor, who stands before him in red cloak and armor, is an altogether lesser figure.

In van Dyck's copy, or rather, reinterpretation on a smaller scale, the center of interest has shifted; the Emperor and not the saint has captured van Dyck's imagination. His Emperor is beardless and wiry, with the hagridden face of a man haunted by sin. The saint, on the other hand, is a much less impressive figure than the heroic prelate of Rubens.

For van Dyck the subject was not—as it was for Rubens—the triumph of the Church and the moral law; he had a more secular interest in the conflicting emotions of the Emperor. Van Dyck's picture is a psychological study, not a moral lesson.

Part of the reason for the confusion between Rubens' work and that of the young van Dyck is that it was Rubens' habit to go over his assistants' finished paintings, adding his own touches. It is thus difficult to establish how much, as a general rule, he left to his assistants. Rubens' large output has given rise to the belief that he merely made the preliminary sketches and touched up the final product, and for this reason the disparaging term "factory" has been applied to his studio. This unsympathetic idea of his methods seems to derive chiefly from the written account of a Danish visitor to Rubens' house in Antwerp. He saw a number of young artists in the studio making full-sized pictures from outlines sketched by the master. Rubens himself was at work on a picture—but was at the same time listening to a reading from a classical book, conversing with his visitors and dictating a letter! Can Rubens have been showing off his multitudinous activities for the benefit of the sightseer? It sounds like it. Paring away the exaggerations, it is probable that he was listening to a reader while he painted (we know from other sources that he often did this) and that a secretary came into the studio with some letters for him to correct and sign. He carried on a large correspondence and was perfectly capable of attending to it while he painted.

But generalizations about his methods cannot be made from a single account. It is clear from Rubens' own letters and comments—as also from the character of his later works—that he was not fully satisfied by this reliance on other hands. From about 1617 to about 1622, when his fame and the number of his orders were rising fast, he did indeed try a sort of "factory" method as a way of satisfying a demand for his work that threatened to exceed the supply. It is noticeable that the period includes the years during which the dexterous and quick-working van Dyck was his principal assistant.

In 1620 van Dyck left Rubens and Antwerp to seek his fortune in England, where he had had a tempting offer to be a court painter; he later moved on to Italy to complete his studies. After his departure Rubens seems to have made less use of assistants to complete his pictures. He had himself acquired such assurance and swiftness of hand during his years of self-imposed training in Italy that it was quicker for him to execute his own ideas than to gear his program to the work of slower and less skilled craftsmen.

The confusion about Rubens' methods of work has been further increased by the failure to distinguish between a variety of different ways in which painters in his time customarily enlisted the help of pupils, assistants or collaborators. Thus, a so-called workshop piece—that is, a painting carried out by pupils under the supervision of a master—would be, generally speaking, inferior to a work executed from the designs of the master by a less experienced but fully qualified painter. Both would differ altogether in quality from a painting executed by

Late in his life, Rubens designed nine woodcuts, one of which, *The Rest on the Flight into Egypt*, is shown here. After the woodcut had been carved in reverse, a "counterproof," or exact image *(above)* was obtained by pressing the freshly inked print to a blank sheet. On such proofs Rubens indicated, in ink washes, the changes he wished his engraver to incise on the woodblock. After six revisions, the artist achieved a final print *(below)* with all the details of light, shadow and line that he desired.

two distinguished masters working in collaboration—a procedure that was very popular in Antwerp.

Rubens often collaborated in this way. His partnership with Brueghel produced about a dozen paintings, one of the most effective of which was an enchanting *Adam and Eve in Paradise.* Brueghel painted a blue-green landscape, alive with all manner of birds and beasts; Rubens added graceful figures of Adam and Eve. Besides his close association with Snyders and van Dyck, Rubens also worked jointly with such lesser-known painters as Jan Wildens, Lucas van Uden and Paul de Vos, all masters in the Guild of St. Luke. Their contributions to Rubens' work consisted largely in painting landscapes and animals for pictures in which he added the figures.

One other kind of working arrangement used by Rubens should be noted. At the end of his life, when he was hampered by failing health, he received a gigantic commission to decorate the King of Spain's hunting lodge. Time was a consideration, as it had been in the commission from the Jesuits. Rubens did what only a painter of his immense prestige and personal influence could have done: he mobilized a group of Antwerp masters to paint a number of the pictures from his designs. This, like the plan for the Jesuit church, was an arrangement designed to meet a special emergency and represented an out-of-the-ordinary procedure. In general it is fair to say that during Rubens' most productive years the majority of his paintings were in every sense his own work.

Within a few years of his return to Antwerp from Italy, Rubens was receiving commissions for pictures from every quarter: from German princes, Genoese bankers, Spanish noblemen and Bavarian aristocrats, from churches in Italy, from the King of France and England's Prince of Wales. In great demand as a religious painter, he was almost equally sought after for portraits and hunting pieces, for pictures of classical and historical subjects.

In the immense population of these classical pictures—the gods and goddesses, warriors and amazons, nymphs and satyrs of antiquity and legend—it is possible sometimes to detect the source from which Rubens borrowed a figure or an idea. Here one can spot the torso of the famous *Laocoön,* there a pose from Michelangelo, a massive Hercules based on a classical statue, a warrior adapted from a Roman relief, or, as in Rubens' magnificent *Battle of the Amazons,* a group reminiscent of Leonardo da Vinci's *Battle of Anghiari.* But the ideas that he borrowed were at once absorbed into his own vision of the antique world: a highly personal vision, scholarly but lively, sensitive but robust—a triumphant expression of the Baroque spirit.

In these paintings of grand historical and mythological themes, Rubens demonstrated superbly his delight in the beauty of the human form, with a marked preference for the supple curves of the female. Michelangelo, whose treatment of the nude he so much admired, had been enthralled by structure and strength, by muscle and sinew. For Rubens the fascination and the challenge was the representation in paint of the tender and perishable beauty of the human skin.

In his book *The Nude,* the distinguished scholar and art historian Sir

Kenneth Clark has graphically described the artist's problem of painting skin: "That strange substance, of a color neither white nor pink, of a texture smooth yet variable, absorbing the light yet reflecting it, delicate yet resilient, flashing and fading, beautiful and pitiful by turns, presents surely the most difficult problem the painter with sticky pigments and smearing brush has ever been called upon to solve; and perhaps only three men, Titian, Rubens, and Renoir, have been sure how it should be done."

Differences of texture fascinated Rubens, and texture is revealed above all by the quality of light and shade. The human skin, especially the petal-like skin of children and young women, is wonderfully responsive to light, and Rubens developed a dazzling virtuosity in painting it. He was able to catch the rhythms and vitality of flesh by painting it as though it were illuminated by a brilliant light that brought out all the subtle variations of color, texture and contour but that cast no harsh or sharp shadows. The technical basis for this achievement was not complicated, but Rubens applied it with consummate skill. He was in the habit of preparing his canvases (or wood panels, for he preferred to paint on wood for smaller pictures) by spreading over them a foundation layer of gesso—plaster of Paris—and then streaking that with a series of quick, broad brushstrokes of a charcoal preparation. In painting an area of skin that was exposed to bright light, he used heavy impasto—a thick application of pigment—which completely covered the preparation ground; but for shadowed areas he painted very lightly and allowed the ground to show through. Thus his shadows have a translucent, insubstantial effect that gives his rendering of skin a particularly luminous quality.

Rubens' technique of flesh painting was to enthrall such masters of the 19th Century as Delacroix and Renoir—the former so much so that he once borrowed a stepladder from a student in a museum at Antwerp so that he could climb up for a closer view of the master's brushwork in a painting on the wall.

Two pictures that especially demonstrate Rubens' skill at depicting human skin are *The Three Graces (pages 159, 162-163)* and *Rape of the Daughters of Leucippus (pages 158, 160-161).* The latter, which illustrates the story of the abduction of two beautiful nymphs by the demigods Castor and Pollux, is particularly effective because the dazzlingly fair skin of the buxom women is thrown into dramatic relief against not only the darker flesh of their swarthy abductors but also the firm, dappled hide of the kidnappers' horses.

Rubens often exploited this dramatic contrast between humans and animals—and the more exotic the animal, the greater the effect. He painted Neptune with the nymph Amphitrite in a setting of coral and seashells with a crocodile, a rhinoceros and a hippopotamus in attendance. A crocodile also occupies the foreground of the graceful group of nymphs and river gods called *The Four Parts of the World.* Clearly, the artistic function of the crocodile was to make a startling contrast between its harsh and scaly hide and the skin of its human companions.

Rubens was deeply interested in painting animals, and in some of his pictures they are of central importance. His use of the crocodile, the rhinoceros and the hippopotamus was probably suggested by the illustrated travel books that he had in his extensive library. Lions, tigers and occasionally a camel or an elephant could be seen in the menageries that were not infrequently owned by European potentates. Horses, dogs and beasts of burden were all around Rubens in Antwerp, while deer and wild boar were hunted not far off in the Ardennes woods.

Whether he drew from nature, from statues or from books, Rubens' animals are very much alive. The superb *Lion Hunt*, which he painted for the Duke of Bavaria, is a pattern of violent motion. The leaping lion shatters the close knot of men and horses like a missile. The picture is almost bisected by the figure of a huntsman who falls from his horse, head downward, in the lion's path. The whole composition is one of Rubens' most extraordinary achievements in the representation of swift and continuous motion. It comes as no surprise to learn that after the tour de force of the *Lion Hunt* Rubens was approached by numerous collectors asking for similar pictures. The astonishing *Hippopotamus Hunt (pages 46-47)* and the *Wolf and Fox Hunt* are no less alive.

One of the pictures he painted in response to a demand for more lions was an impressive portrayal of *Daniel in the Lions' Den,* a picture that he offered, together with a number of other paintings, in exchange for a collection of Greek and Roman sculpture belonging to Sir Dudley Carleton, English ambassador to The Hague. Carleton, who was a famous patron and collector, agreed to the suggestion with flattering warmth, hailing Rubens as "prince of painters and painter of princes." Rubens refused to accept so grand a title; he was far from being a prince, he said; he was simply a man who lived by the work of his own hands. In spite of his growing wealth and fame, or perhaps because of it, he liked to emphasize that his art was essentially just a craft, a form of skilled manual labor.

Partly through Carleton's interest, Rubens' fame had reached England, and the artist began a productive association with that country and some of its most illustrious figures that was to last the rest of his life. The Prince of Wales, who later became the luckless Charles I, acquired a Rubens *Lion Hunt* for his personal collection in 1621. It was tentatively suggested that Rubens might cross the Channel to decorate the royal Banqueting House, which the celebrated architect Inigo Jones was then building in Whitehall. Rubens was delighted at the prospect, and in commenting on it in a letter to an English acquaintance in Brussels he made a revealing statement about his own personality. "Regarding the hall in the New Palace," he wrote, "I confess that I am by natural instinct better fitted to execute very large works than small curiosities. Everyone according to his gifts; my talent is such that no undertaking, however vast in size or varied in subject, has ever surpassed my courage."

Unfortunately, the Banqueting House was far from finished and for some years no more was heard of this exciting proposal. But in the meantime, an English noblewoman, the Countess of Arundel, asked to have her portrait done as she passed through Antwerp in 1620. Rubens had no need to supplement his income by regular portrait painting, and as a general rule painted only his family, his personal friends or people for whom he had a particular respect. But he granted the Countess' request because her husband was an outstanding patron, "an evangelist of art," as Rubens described him, and also because he was an influential statesman who was known to favor good relations between England and the Spanish Netherlands.

He decided to paint her ladyship in the grand manner, seated in an Italianate setting and accompanied by her dog, her jester and her dwarf (it was fashionable then, and had been since Roman times, for noble personages to keep dwarfs as entertainers and, often, as scapegoats). But the Countess had only a few days to spare, and Rubens could not immediately procure a large enough canvas for the commission. He solved the problem with his usual resourcefulness. In two sittings he painted her head on one canvas, and the heads of the fool, the dwarf and the dog on another. He also sketched the general composition of the group for her approval. After she had gone he secured the proper size canvas and copied what he had done in the sketches. The result *(pages 20-21)* is a dignified yet natural group of a grande dame and her attendants.

Lady Arundel came from one of the oldest and noblest families in England but she was not much to look at. She poked her head forward in an awkward way; despite her grand clothes she seemed ill at ease. Rubens did not flatter her. He made her look well bred and virtuous; he also made her look unmistakably English. She had none of the glamor of the Genoese and Mantuan ladies he had painted in his youth. But anyone who has ever seen a shy Englishwoman anxiously opening a Red Cross bazaar will recognize Lady Arundel at once. Actually, the most interesting figures are the dwarf and the fool, particularly the dwarf, who is richly dressed and has the confident swagger of one who has got on in the world. Somewhat later, Rubens added another figure in the background, sometimes identified as his friend Dudley Carleton, with whom he had exchanged works of art in 1618.

Not only as a painter but also as a collector and connoisseur, Rubens now had connections with princes, bishops, diplomats, prelates and other men of influence throughout Europe. It was partly because of these contacts and partly because of his personal qualifications that Archduke Albert and Archduchess Isabella decided that their court painter might serve them usefully in another function. Recognizing his intelligence and discretion, they conceived that Rubens, under cover of his esthetic interests, could be usefully employed on secret diplomatic missions. The royal couple thus initiated a new phase of his extraordinary career.

The need for diplomacy had become urgent as the international situation had darkened. The Twelve Years' Truce of 1609 between the Spanish Netherlands and their Dutch neighbors to the north was drawing to a close. But this was only a part of a larger scene. Europe was divided into mutually suspicious groups: those states, mainly Catholic, that favored the Habsburg dynasty, and those that for political, economic or religious reasons feared and opposed it. The Habsburg power did indeed overshadow Europe—and more than Europe. The several branches of the dynasty, closely tied by intermarriage, controlled Spain and

Portugal, as well as all the Spanish and Portuguese overseas possessions on the coast of Africa, in India, in the Americas and the Caribbean; they also controlled Southern Italy and Sicily, Austria, Bohemia and part of Hungary. They exercised an influence over all of Germany because the many individual German states were loosely bound together in the so-called Holy Roman Empire (an anachronistic designation inherited from the Middle Ages) and the Emperor was invariably a member of the Habsburg family.

Such concentration of power in the hands of one dynasty was enough to cause anxiety to the sovereigns of England, France, Denmark and Sweden, especially as the kingdom of France—usually the opponent and counterweight to Habsburg ambitions—was at this time economically weak and politically divided. A further dangerous element was added to the situation by the religious division that had already caused so much fighting in Europe during the last century. The Habsburg dynasty had evolved a tradition of championing the Catholic Church, and it was generally feared in Germany and Central Europe that a new attack on Protestants was imminent in all states under Habsburg influence.

In an attempt to forestall this eventuality the Protestants of Bohemia revolted against their Habsburg monarch in May 1618. They rushed the castle of Prague and threw the Emperor's governors out of an upper-story window (miraculously none of the three men thus mishandled sustained any serious injury). In due course the rebel government elected a new Protestant king. He was Frederick V, a German prince from the Rhineland, married to the only daughter of King James I of England. The Bohemians hoped, of course, to gain the alliance of other German Protestant princes and of the English King. But they miscalculated. Fearing to precipitate a general European war, the German princes and the King of England hung back. In 1620 Frederick V was overwhelmingly defeated by the Habsburg forces at the Battle of the White Mountain, a few miles beyond the gates of Prague. The Bohemian uprising ended and Bohemian Protestantism was ruthlessly crushed. The hapless King Frederick could not even return to his Rhineland home: the Spaniards had occupied it.

These events were the prelude to the confused and terrible struggle known as the Thirty Years' War, which eventually involved all the European powers in devastating conflict.

Where did the Netherlands stand in all these swirling religious and nationalistic crosscurrents? The Northern provinces, which had revolted from Spain and set themselves up as the Dutch Republic, stood squarely against Habsburg aggression. It was not only a matter of religion; the expanding world trade of the Dutch brought them into collision with Spanish overseas power. If they should be reconquered, their trade as well as their freedom would be extinguished. Therefore, they received with open arms the fugitive Frederick V, not with any intention of restoring him to Bohemia—a hopeless task—but in the hope of expelling the Spanish troops who had entrenched themselves in his lands on the Rhine, uncomfortably close at hand.

The Archduke Albert, the Archduchess Isabella and their loyal subjects in the Spanish Netherlands were of course on the Habsburg side. Albert came from the imperial Austrian branch of the dynasty; Isabella was the daughter of the previous King of Spain, Philip II, and half-sister of the present King Philip III. Naturally, as good Catholics, Rubens and other loyalists could not but applaud the victory won at Prague over rebellious Protestant heretics.

But as a civilized man Rubens feared the dreadful effects of renewed war, either between his nation and the Dutch or among the other nations of Europe. Perhaps the fatal moves could yet be prevented? The truce between the Spanish Netherlands and the Dutch Republic was running out; but the Archduke and his wife, not realizing how injurious it would be to Dutch prosperity and prospects, still hoped that the Hollanders would rejoin the fold, or at least agree to a peaceful settlement. Rubens, who had useful contacts in the North, proved to be a valuable and discreet intermediary in secret overtures that were made at this time to the Prince of Orange. It was suggested, on behalf of the Spanish Crown, that the Prince should become hereditary ruler of the Dutch provinces, accepting the overlordship of Spain, if he would agree to a peace with the Southern Netherlands.

The suggestion, though sincerely intended for the preservation of peace, was in fact misguided. Prince Maurice, general of the armies of the Dutch Republic and the effective leader of its people for almost all his adult life, was ambitious and could be ruthless. He had recently crushed a dangerous religious controversy in the Dutch provinces in the interests of national unity and strength. He ruled with great authority but he was essentially a soldier—at this time probably the best in Europe. He was also a realist in politics. Great as his influence was, he held his office by election and he knew that he could never carry the Dutch people with him if he seriously entertained an offer to subjugate them to the King of Spain. Furthermore, his personal honor and obligations also spoke against such an action. His father, William the Silent, had led the original Dutch revolt. Maurice had inherited the task and from his earliest manhood had successfully championed the cause of the rising Republic. A lifetime of such service is not lightly thrown away.

Little is known of these negotiations or of the precise details of the part Rubens played, but it is clear that both his advice and his diplomatic skill were used by the Archduke and the Archduchess in the preliminary moves. It was his first essay in secret diplomacy and was to be followed by many more. But it was inevitable that the Prince of Orange would reject his southern neighbors' offer of peace at such a price. To have done anything else would have been to betray everything for which he and his father had fought.

The Archduke and the Archduchess were no less bound than Maurice of Orange to continue to fight for what they believed to be the just rights of the hereditary rulers of the Netherlands. As they saw it, the rebellious North, the so-called Dutch Republic, must be reunited with the loyal South. Thus, in 1621, the Twelve Years' Truce expired, and war began again between the neighboring and kindred countries.

Rubens would not live to see the end of it.

Frederick V, the luckless German Prince who unwittingly launched the Thirty Years' War, was the subject of dozens of political cartoons, like this one of 1621, satirizing his meteoric rise and fall. Frederick, who became King of Protestant Bohemia and then quickly lost his crown in battle against the Catholic Habsburgs, is shown being helped up the wheel of fortune by two of his advisers, then sitting briefly as king before being toppled. At right he is rescued in the nets of Dutch fishermen, a reference to his exile in Protestant Holland, governed by his uncle.

The Antwerp Masters

As Rubens' fame increased and commissions poured in, he found it necessary to develop a staff whose job it was to prepare canvases, mix paints and keep the studio running smoothly. It is not known how many students Rubens had; as a court painter he was free from the usual guild tax on such helpers and was not obliged to keep records of them. He must have had quite a few, however, because shortly after he opened his studio in 1611 he wrote to a friend saying that he could accept no one else, having already had to refuse over 100 applicants.

Under Rubens' guidance, pupils made copies of his popular paintings, executed works that the master had roughed out (he would later retouch them), and prepared tapestry designs in color from his drawings. The few who were skilled in engraving and woodcutting helped to produce the flow of prints whose wide European sale contributed to Rubens' wealth and fame.

Apart from the highly talented painter Anthony van Dyck (one of his works is shown at right), few of Rubens' pupils rose to fame. However, Rubens collaborated often with Jan Brueghel and Frans Snyders, independently established masters whose specialized assistance—landscape, still-life and animal subjects—enabled him to produce many of the large, richly detailed paintings for which he became famous. Fine painters in their own right, these men, and Rubens' friend Jacob Jordaens, established 17th Century Antwerp as a leading center for art.

A superlative portraitist, Anthony van Dyck was chief court painter to England's Charles I for more than five years, during which he produced this study of the monarch and many likenesses of British nobility. In appreciation of his art, Charles knighted the Flemish painter, provided him with both a winter and a summer residence, and awarded him a handsome annual pension.

Anthony van Dyck: *Portrait of Charles I at the Hunt*, 1635

Anthony van Dyck: *Portrait of James Stuart, Duke of Lennox and Richmond,* c. 1632-1640

Anthony van Dyck: *Portrait of Marie-Louise de Tassis*, c. 1630

Van Dyck was not only an extremely facile painter —he often worked on as many as three portraits at once, admitting sitters to his studio for one-hour sessions—but an unusually perceptive one. In portraits, which became his specialty, he invariably captured more than a simple likeness. Van Dyck's elegant and assured style, perfectly suited to the attitudes affected by such gentlemen as James Stuart *(left)*, was the model in English portraiture for many years. And in paintings of beautiful women, like the one shown above, his attention to details of costume and the perfection of complexion and features reveals as much about the lady as her shyly seductive glance.

Frans Snyders, one of Rubens' frequent collaborators, became the first specialist in a new and peculiarly Flemish form of still life. Akin to the hunting scenes that Rubens was popularizing, Snyders' animal still lifes contained a hint of action—a flapping hen, a squealing piglet, a sniffing dog. But principally they enabled the painter to demonstrate his skill at composing a rich variety of textures, colors and shapes.

Snyders, who assisted Rubens with animals in several large hunting scenes, was an accomplished painter of both living and dead game (although Rubens justly felt himself superior to Snyders in painting beasts in action). Having studied with Pieter Bruegel's painter-sons (who were landscape and still-life specialists), Snyders made the traditional pilgrimage to Italy but returned to Antwerp to pursue his career.

In addition to his masterful treatment of objects—he could paint anything from a grape to a swan with verisimilitude—Snyders had a fine feeling for large, well-balanced compositions, as can be seen in the work at right. The expressive features of the old vendor and the excited boy in this picture show that Snyders could also paint the human animal convincingly.

Frans Snyders: *The Game Vendor*, date unknown

Jan Brueghel: *Scent*, c. 1617

Jan Brueghel, a son of the Flemish master Pieter Bruegel, resumed the historical spelling of the family name, carried on his father's tradition of landscape painting and made a specialty of floral still lifes.

At a time when Rubens and Snyders were filling huge still lifes with game, fruits and plants, Jan Brueghel preferred tightly composed and beautifully delicate flower studies. Occasionally, as in the large painting here (from a series on the senses), he combined landscape and floral studies in monumental conceptions peopled with allegorical figures.

Brueghel was a student of nature, searching widely for flower specimens that he painted from life. He usually worked on floral pieces in the spring. Toward the end of summer, when no more good flowering plants were to be had, he would paint landscapes.

Brueghel found a wide audience among discriminating collectors. One of them, an Italian cardinal, observed: "Even the most insignificant works of Jan Brueghel show how much grace and spirit there is in his art. One can admire at the same time its greatness and its delicacy."

91

Although he never collaborated directly with Rubens, Jacob Jordaens was a close friend and colleague, and the leading painter in Antwerp after the master's death in 1640. Jordaens had, in fact, completed three paintings left unfinished by Rubens, who, during his last years of life, was severely afflicted with gout. It was Jordaens who finished part of his colleague's last great commission, a lengthy series of mythological scenes for the hunting lodge of Spain's Philip IV, the Torre de la Parada.

Some of Jordaens' early work seems to have been influenced by Rubens' own style, as is evidenced, for example, by the smooth finish and almost sculptural modeling of the figures in the painting shown below at right. But in sum, the two painters were as different as they could be, seeming almost to represent the two mainstreams of Flemish art. Rubens, on the one hand,

Jacob Jordaens: *The Satyr and the Peasant*, 1620

was a pure painter, interested in exploiting the sensuous materials of life with what appear to be unlimited resources of color and brushwork. On the other hand, Jordaens, while a masterful technician, preferred to narrow his focus, often repeating satisfactory figures and compositions, and always insisting on telling his story straight—and it is often a moral or didactic story. In the painting shown at left, Jordaens pictured an old satyr pointing out how incongruous it is for the peasant to blow on his soup to cool it, when he may, at another time, blow on his hands to warm them. The figures from this homespun allegory, based on one of Aesop's fables that Jordaens painted several times, also appear in various other genre and religious scenes. Limited in imagination and daring, but skilled in his craft, Jordaens helped fill the gap left by Rubens competently, if without genius.

Jacob Jordaens: *The Four Evangelists*, c. 1625

The Master's Studio

Rubens' studio, where van Dyck and Snyders worked as associates, and where Antwerp's other talented painters frequently visited, was built as an annex to the house he purchased about 1610 *(pages 26 and 27)*. An upper floor, reached by the staircase seen rising above the vestibule in the background, served Rubens' pupils; the main floor was reserved for the master himself. There, with tall windows providing ample daylight, Rubens could work on as many as three large compositions at once—the room is 36 feet long and nearly 26 feet across. Sometimes, however, Rubens and his assistants merely did the preliminary painting in the studio, waiting until the canvas was delivered to the client before adding the finishing touches. The Marie de' Medici paintings, for example, were completed in this fashion, in Paris. In other instances, when Rubens was working with an established collaborator like Jan Brueghel, the canvas was probably sent to Brueghel's studio and later returned to Rubens for completion.

The studio apparently became something of an Antwerp showplace during Rubens' lifetime; the painter seems almost to have anticipated this by planning a small gallery on the staircase landing, where visitors could stand overlooking the work below without disturbing progress. Privileged guests were also permitted to visit the pupils' room upstairs, where the assistants might be seen at their tasks. Among such distinguished visitors were the Archduchess Isabella, Marie de' Medici and the Duke of Buckingham, all of whom owned paintings by Rubens and were probably curious to see his studio.

V

Public Fortune, Private Grief

Henry IV gazes tenderly at his Queen, Marie de' Medici, in one of Rubens' oil sketches for a cycle of paintings depicting Henry's life, a series commissioned by Marie but never completed. Sketches like these, loosely brushed in pale colors—pinks, blues and browns —often served the artist as models for his larger works.

Henry IV and Marie de' Medici, before 1625

The five years following the resumption of war with the Dutch in 1621 were strenuous ones for Rubens. He became more deeply involved in public affairs as he was called upon several times to serve his country in search of peace. His immense artistic output still continued to expand, and he undertook one of the most demanding commissions of his career. He also suffered a personal blow that put a sad, sudden end to his happy domestic tranquillity.

But for the first year or so of the war he pursued his painting and enjoyed his family with little interruption, although at times the military operations were close enough to Antwerp for him to hear in his studio the reverberation of the cannon.

His fame had by this time spread far beyond the Spanish Netherlands, helped by the sale of the engravings whose production he had supervised with so much care. Most of the leading connoisseurs of Europe possessed one or more original works from his hand—a great hunting piece, some glowing mythological subject or perhaps a scene from the Old Testament. His former patrons in Genoa, among others, ordered designs for tapestries that were woven on the looms of Brussels. His altarpieces illuminated churches in Italy and Germany as well as throughout the Netherlands.

His fellow citizens of Antwerp not infrequently referred to him as "the Apelles of our age"—giving him the name of the most famous Greek painter of antiquity. He brought custom as well as fame to the city. Travelers with any pretensions to an interest in the arts frequently made a detour by Antwerp to visit Rubens' collection of pictures and statues and to catch a glimpse of him at work in his studio.

Success brings with it much facile praise and an unrelenting demand on the creative gifts of the artist; the two together can weaken the faculties of self-criticism and exhaust the imaginative powers. But Rubens rarely fell below his own high standards, and never ran out of ideas or lacked the energy to carry them through. At the height of his fame he brought to each new undertaking the same qualities of concentration and enthusiasm that he had given to his earliest works in Italy. He truly loved his craft and seems never to have suffered from the staleness and frustration that so often beset even the greatest of creative artists.

Rubens' nephew Philip, who spent much of his youth in his uncle's care, left a vivid account of how the artist organized his daily life, fitting work, exercise, recreation and regular religious observances into a full day. He rose at four every morning to hear Mass. Then he breakfasted and went to his studio. He stayed at work until about five in the afternoon, but the long day was often enlivened by the arrival of visitors with whom he conversed while painting. When there were no visitors he sometimes dictated his correspondence, or listened to readings from his favorite authors. (In books Rubens had a wide, discriminating taste, enjoying writers of many different opinions and religions. He particularly valued antiquarian works and books of travel for the information and ideas in them that quickly fired his visual imagination.)

He ate little during working hours; the usual 17th Century snack was some bread and cheese, to which Rubens added fruit from his garden when it was in season. The main meal, the family dinner, came at the end of the working day; no doubt it was a solid repast in the Flemish manner with roast meat or fish, egg dishes, solid pastries and pies—washed down with a liberal supply of local beer or wine from France or the Rhineland. But Rubens himself ate and drank with moderation. In the evening, in summer, he went out for fresh air and exercise, walking or more often riding. He was a good and graceful horseman and was by now rich enough to keep fine mounts. Two horses that appear several times in his pictures—a dapple-gray with a long tail and a noble bay with a white blaze on its forehead—were probably favorites from his own stable.

Since his studio was open to clients and friends, Rubens seldom went out, except to visit the studios of other painters in whose work he was interested or to make calls at the houses of a chosen few. Among his closest friends were Nicolas Rockox, the learned burgomaster of Antwerp, Caspar Gevaerts, a distinguished scholar and antiquarian, and his old schoolfellow Balthasar Moretus, head of the Plantin press. He painted fine portraits of Rockox and Gevaerts; he put his talents at the service of Moretus not only by designing title pages and illustrations for his books, but also by devising and carrying out a scheme of decoration for his house, painting a series of portraits for each of the principal rooms, beginning with members of the Plantin-Moretus family and going on to saints and sages of the past.

Another family with whom he was on terms of warm friendship was that of a silk and tapestry merchant, Daniel Fourment, who lived close by with an exuberant brood of four sons and seven daughters. The eldest of these daughters was Susanna, an attractive girl with a slender, pointed face and large lively eyes. She was painted several times by both Rubens and van Dyck. The most famous and most attractive of the portraits by Rubens is the so-called *Chapeau de Paille—The Straw Hat*. (Actually the hat is a felt beaver, fashionable at the time; some scholars think the source of confusion lies in the word *paille*, which means "straw" in French now, but which in earlier times also had the sense of "canopy"; other historians feel that the name, which was not Rubens' own choice but was applied later, is simply a mistake: under dark varnish, to a careless eye, the hat may have looked like straw.) The hat's wide, dark brim enhances the clarity of Susanna's complexion and the brilliance of her eyes. It is an open-air picture, with no background except the sky, and it seems bathed in the transparent light of springtime.

Susanna's youngest sister, Hélène, promised to be the beauty of the family. It is likely that Rubens, who rarely missed a chance to sketch anything, animate or inanimate, that stirred his visual fancy, noted the gestures and features of this pretty little girl. A long-standing tradition has it that he painted her at the age of about 10 as the model for the Virgin Mary in his picture *The Education of the Virgin.*

The long hours that he worked did not prevent Rubens from leading a full domestic life. His eldest child, Clara Serena, seems to have inherited much of her mother's sweetness of character, while his son Albert early showed a bent for antiquarian study that pleased his father. Isabella Rubens presided with unfailing good humor over the large household. As well as supervising the nursery and other domestic affairs, she was responsible for arranging that the master's table was always well-supplied and equal to the demands of visitors and the appetites of the hungry young men working in the studio. In her own sphere she worked as hard as her husband. Some of his patrons recognized this and sent her presents, such as valuable jewelry or, in one case, an elegant pair of gloves.

Though these years, the early 1620s, were happy and productive ones for Rubens, it was an unsettled time for his country. In 1621, a few weeks after the end of the truce, Archduke Albert died. The event altered the political status of the Spanish Netherlands. When the Archduke and Archduchess took over the government in 1598 it had been hoped that a son would succeed them as independent sovereign of the Netherlands. But no son had been born and, with the Archduke's death, the sovereignty reverted to the King of Spain. This did not at first appear to make much difference, because Philip IV immediately appointed the Archduchess to govern the Netherlands on his behalf. Her intelligence and ability had always made her an equal partner with her husband, so continuity of policy was assured. But she was 55, an age that was thought of as old in those days. Her death would confirm the dependence of the Spanish Netherlands on the far-away court in Madrid and might place the country in the hands of some unknown and perhaps incompetent Spanish nominee. Before that happened it was to be hoped that peace with the Dutch would be restored and the prosperity of the country reestablished on a firmer footing.

When her husband died the Archduchess adopted the dress of a nun, and wore it the rest of her life. It was in this habit that she posed for Rubens when he painted her official portrait in 1625. Public figures then were not so acutely conscious as they are now of their "image," yet the more intelligent of them took some trouble to create the right impression by carefully selecting and controlling the portraits that were to be copied, engraved and sold to their subjects. Rubens painted the Archduchess without flattery; he showed her as a heavily built middle-aged nun, whose strong features lack conventional beauty. Yet she is clearly no ordinary or commonplace person: the eyes miss nothing, the mouth is firm and judicious, the expression is one of authority. It is a face that inspires confidence and respect—and that precisely was what the Archduchess wished and deserved to inspire in her people.

Her principal adviser, now that war with the Dutch had begun again, was the general of her armed forces, Ambrogio Spinola, a Genoese professional soldier. It was not unusual in those times of ill-defined national loyalties for rulers to employ foreign-born generals; the principal object was to secure the ablest soldier available, regardless of his place of birth.

Rubens, as loyal citizen and trusted servant of the Archduchess, was deeply concerned with all developments in the affairs of state. He was later to admit that he had at one time somewhat distrusted Spinola's alien influence in the Netherlands, but he soon came to recognize his virtues. He described him to a friend as "a man of great prudence and discretion," but added a little ruefully that he "knew no more about [painting] than a porter." Spinola nonetheless commissioned works from Rubens and valued him as a keen observer of public affairs. His portrait, done by Rubens at about this time, shows him standing ramrod straight, hand on sword, looking at the spectator with wary, observant eyes.

Italian architecture was one of Rubens' many interests, and in 1621 he published *Palazzi di Genova*, a book of engravings illustrating dozens of fine houses in Genoa. In addition to façade designs and cutaway views like those shown here, the book contained detailed floor plans to guide any housebuilders in Antwerp who shared Rubens' enthusiasm for the Italian style.

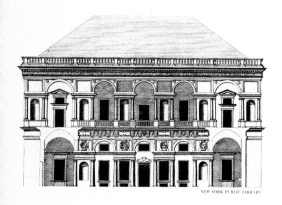

Rubens' duties as a court painter sometimes interrupted his more serious work; he and Jan Brueghel were sent for hurriedly to decorate a suite of rooms in the palace at Brussels when the King of Poland's eldest son was expected on a visit. Then after the Prince arrived he had to be received and personally conducted around the Rubens studio and collection of antiquities. A portrait to mark the occasion was also required.

But much more important work was soon to come. Rubens was disappointed to have heard nothing more about the decoration of the King of England's new Banqueting House in Whitehall. He had been excited at the prospect because the building was in the classic Palladian architectural style of Italy, which he admired no less than Italian painting. He had been delighted with the opportunity to decorate the huge new Jesuit church of Antwerp, also a modern building in the Italian style. But he longed for the chance to enrich a great secular building in the same way —to glorify some northern palace as Titian, Tintoretto and Veronese had glorified the great palaces of Venice.

Rubens had himself tried to set a new fashion in domestic architecture in the Netherlands with the Italianate additions he had made to his own house. He was also preparing for publication a number of engravings of the principal palaces of Genoa, which he hoped would serve as examples for northern architects and would help to replace what he described as the "barbaric or gothic" style with more spacious classical buildings.

It was therefore with the keenest enthusiasm that he accepted in the fall of 1621 an offer to decorate the magnificent residence that the Queen Mother of France was building in Paris. The Luxembourg Palace when completed would certainly be one of the finest examples of the Italian manner north of the Alps; the task of decorating it, which was to occupy much of Rubens' time for the next three years, was a worthy challenge to his enormous creative energy.

The Queen Mother was Marie de' Medici, the Florentine Princess whose wedding Rubens had attended while working for the Duke of Mantua more than 20 years before. She had led an eventful life since that time. Her husband, King Henry IV, had been assassinated in 1610, leaving her as Regent for her young son Louis XIII. A silly, willful woman, possessive and greedy for power, she had been much influenced by flattering and ill-chosen favorites. One of them, a Florentine adventurer named Concino Concini, controlled the French government for seven years. Then in 1617 the 16-year-old Louis arranged the murder of Concini, assumed the government himself and exiled his mother from his court. Despite this unfilial behavior, Louis XIII was by nature affectionate and by training pious; he did not wish to live at enmity with his mother, provided she desisted from political intrigue. A reconciliation took place and by 1621 she was back in Paris, spending a fortune on her palatial new residence.

The job she had in mind for Rubens was the decoration of the palace's two huge ceremonial galleries. In the first hall there were to be 21 paintings devoted to the virtues and achievements of her own life. Illustrations of the career of her husband King Henry IV would decorate the second gallery; the details for that commission would be arranged later. Henry had been a great king, probably the greatest France was ever to know, but his widow typically put herself first.

Rubens traveled to Paris early in 1622 to consult the architect of the palace, Salomon de Brosse, and to settle the terms of the contract. Archduchess Isabella was by no means displeased to have him go, for she was anxious to cultivate the goodwill of the French court. She entrusted Rubens with greetings and gifts—including, for the Queen Mother, a pretty little lap dog in a jeweled collar.

Rubens himself looked forward to the opportunity of meeting new friends in France, especially various scholars with whom he already corresponded. The age of specialization had not yet dawned. Scholars at this time, like their forerunners in the Renaissance, often pursued a variety of different interests—science, the literature, art and philosophy as well as the customs of antiquity, and often also the past history of their own countries. In the absence of the learned journals that today disseminate erudite speculation and discovery, scholars wrote freely to one another about their questions, theories and findings. Thus Rubens was at one time consulted by the English antiquarian Camden about a statue dug up in England and thought to represent the Egyptian goddess Isis; and he was one of the many scholars with whom Pierre Dupuy, the royal librarian in Paris, maintained a voluminous correspondence. This particularly pleased Rubens, for he reserved his highest admiration for the learning and literature of France, which was rapidly supplanting Italy as the intellectual center of Europe. "France contains within itself the flower of the world," he once wrote to Dupuy.

The intellectual community in Paris accepted Rubens with equal pleasure and respect. He was particularly welcomed by the prestigious antiquarian Nicolas-Claude Fabri de Peiresc, who could not speak too highly of Rubens' learning, his deep knowledge of Classical antiquity, his charm and good sense. "He was born to please and delight, in all that he

Artists and weavers of the 17th Century often combined their talents to produce superb tapestries such as *The Marriage of Constantine and Fausta*, executed from a design by Rubens. It is part of a series of 12 tapestries on the life of the Roman Emperor commissioned by King Louis XIII of France in 1622. For each one Rubens prepared an oil sketch; weavers in Paris then reproduced in cloth the subtleties of contour and line that Rubens had created in paint, as seen in the detail *(below)* of Fausta's father and an older spectator.

does or says," Peiresc wrote. A lifelong friendship was quickly cemented as Rubens and Peiresc discussed innumerable topics of learning and taste, ranging from Roman cameos to medieval manuscripts, from modern literature to the problem of perpetual motion—an exercise in dynamics that fascinated educated men in the 17th Century.

Interviews between Rubens and the Queen Mother were, in their own way, equally satisfactory. Rubens returned to Antwerp after a few weeks with a handsome contract for 20,000 crowns and a mind teeming with ideas for the series of Medici paintings. He had also received a separate commission from King Louis for the designs for several tapestries telling the story of Constantine, the Roman Emperor who became a Christian. Constantine, according to an ancient legend, had been victorious in battle in the year 312 because he had been directed by a vision that appeared in the heavens—with the words *In hoc signo vinces:* "Under this sign thou shalt conquer"—to take the Cross for his banner. Raised to power by divine intervention, he had used his power to establish the true Church throughout the Roman Empire. For pious Roman Catholic princes of the Counter Reformation, this was an inspiring theme because it emphasized the unity of interest between church and state. It also lent itself to effective decorative treatment, with an elaborate display of Roman warriors, banners, horses and architecture.

Rubens soon set to work on both commissions for the French court. The preliminary sketches for the life of Marie de' Medici were ready within two months; those for the Constantine tapestry series followed soon after. Both were received with approval in Paris, though a few critical voices were raised because some of the Roman horsemen in the Constantine series appeared to be bowlegged. A tendency to this malformation is common among those who spend their lives in the saddle, but this stroke of realism, very typical of Rubens, was felt by some of the French purists to be incompatible with the dignity of the subject. Quite possibly some of the criticism could be blamed, too, on the envy that Rubens' appointment had inspired in some of the French painters who had been passed over for the commission.

That enmity may also have inspired the malicious circulation in Paris of a rumor of Rubens' death. Rubens, alive and well in Antwerp, made light of it, but the report was based on a circumstance that could have had tragic results. The successful collaboration between Rubens and Lucas Vorsterman, the engraver, had been going on for four or five years. Vorsterman was an exceptionally sensitive craftsman who understood how to render in his own medium the delicate gradations of light and shade that were characteristic of Rubens. But the extreme technical virtuosity and concentration required for this precise artistry imposed a heavy strain on Vorsterman, who was a man of nervous and apparently paranoiac temperament.

It seems that the effort to complete one of the finest of his prints— taken from Rubens' *The Fall of the Rebel Angels*—precipitated a mental collapse. Vorsterman became moody, hostile and so morbidly jealous that he threatened to kill Rubens. The Archduchess had to appoint a special guard to protect the painter until Vorsterman left the country. Removed from the source of his obsessions, the engraver recovered, did some good work in England and later returned to Antwerp.

Meanwhile the enormous pictures for the Medici gallery *(pages 109-119)* were approaching completion. Rubens needed all his rich vocabulary of emblems and his knowledge of Classical mythology to fill the 21 canvases with scenes complimentary to the life of the Queen Mother. He and his friend Peiresc corresponded at length on the problem; Peiresc discussed the suitability of various ideas and images, and warned Rubens of the dangers of giving political offense. The Queen's career could be safely treated only in very general terms. Rubens abandoned one picture —depicting her flight from Paris after her quarrel with her son—and substituted an allegorical theme, *The Blessings of the Regency (page 117)*. In this, as he told Peiresc, he depicted "the flowering of the Kingdom of France, with the revival of the sciences and the arts through the liberality and the splendor of Her Majesty, who sits upon a shining throne and holds a scale in her hands, keeping the world in equilibrium by her prudence and equity." *That*, at any rate, was sure to please.

The flow of visual imagination never failed Rubens, whether he was treating a scene in allegorical or in realistic terms. The pictures devoted to the Queen's birth and education *(page 110)* showed her surrounded by the Graces, and such suitable divinities as Mercury and Apollo. Other subjects were careful reconstructions of historical truth. Rubens painted Marie's marriage in Florence—*The Marriage by Proxy (page 111)*— much as he remembered it. *The Coronation of Marie (pages 114-115)* is a superb representation of a gorgeous ceremony. The kneeling figure of the Queen fills the center of the composition. On either side of her stand her son and daughter, and a venerable prelate holds the crown above her head. Behind the Queen are her trainbearers and maids of honor, lovely young women whose faces rise like flowers from the stiff and shimmering lace and brocade of their sumptuous clothes. Next to this group stands a magnificently dressed older woman who contemplates the kneeling Queen with a look combining regret and resignation. This is Marguerite de Valois, first wife of King Henry IV, who had borne him no heir, and who had agreed to an annulment to make way for her successor. The King himself is seen watching the ceremony from above.

In other pictures of the series Rubens mingled allegory and realism. Thus *The Birth of Louis XIII (page 111)* shows the Queen flanked by such symbolical figures as Justice and Fecundity, while the newborn infant is in somewhat alarming proximity to a serpent, a symbol of Health. But the Queen herself is realistically drawn, propped up, gazing at her son with that mingled expression of exhaustion, love and triumph characteristic of a newly delivered mother. She has scuffed her slippers off her plump bare feet. A tiny lap dog in the foreground is a portrait of the pet that Rubens had brought her as a present from Archduchess Isabella.

Rubens finished the first nine Medici paintings in 1623. He delivered them—overland, by wagon—to Paris in May of that year and spent a month putting them in their frames, though they would not be finally installed in the palace until all 21 were finished. The Queen Mother, for all her faults, came from a family of outstanding patrons of art, and she

Rubens, an avid collector of antique art objects, greatly admired the Cameo of Tiberius (above), which he saw in Paris in 1622. Carved some time in the First Century on a piece of sardonyx a foot high, the cameo shows the Roman Emperor sitting with his mother Livia and receiving the warrior Germanicus. Rubens was so impressed by the cameo's design that he first made a drawing of it (below), filling in damaged areas as he imagined they had been, and later made an engraving and a painting.

took a genuine interest in the progress of the pictures. While Rubens was framing the canvases she enjoyed visiting and talking to him. No doubt they conversed in her native Italian tongue, which he spoke much more fluently than French.

On these visits the Queen Mother sometimes took along her youngest child, the graceful 13-year-old Princess Henrietta Maria. Before Rubens returned to Paris two years later with the remaining 12 paintings, the Princess was betrothed to King Charles I of England and Rubens heard that she was impatient to see him before she left for her new home. He was pleased at this enthusiasm from his little admirer, and sent the encouraging news that her future husband was, in his opinion, "the greatest amateur of paintings among the princes of the world."

As it happened, Rubens reached Paris with the last Medici pictures in February 1625, three months before the Princess' wedding. He spent the time framing, retouching and altering the paintings and overseeing their installation in the palace. His commission finished on time, he was present at Henrietta Maria's nuptials as he had been at her mother's a quarter of a century before.

Despite everything that was going on in Paris during these busy weeks, Rubens, as always, found time for fresh observation and study. He visited the studios of other painters, and copied some of the decorations in fresco and stucco at the Fontainebleau Palace, designed in the previous century by the Italian artist Primaticcio (who had also helped decorate Mantua's Palazzo del Te). In addition, Rubens consulted with his friend Peiresc about plans for a book on Greek and Roman gems; it was agreed that Rubens would draw the pictures and Peiresc would write the text.

Of more immediate practical interest to Rubens were his discussions with the Luxembourg Palace architect, Salomon de Brosse, about the size and number of pictures needed for the second gallery, whose decoration would be devoted to the life of King Henry IV. Rubens was enthusiastically looking forward to his work on this series. It was a theme, he wrote, "so vast and magnificent that it would suffice for ten galleries." In the scenes of conflict and triumph that he was already planning, he would not be cumbered with the puddinglike Marie de' Medici as his central figure, but would have as a subject the virile and attractive King. When depicting the King in the Medici series, Rubens had had only the help of a plaster cast taken from a bronze statue. From this not very promising material he had already created, in preliminary paintings for the new series, a convincing image of Henry as a taut, powerful, wiry man, a dominating personality and presence.

But Rubens' eagerness to get into full stride on the second series was checked almost before the first series was in place. The architectural plans for the second gallery were not yet approved. Delays and obstructions began to occur. It was rumored that Cardinal Richelieu, the able, ambitious prelate who had recently become the chief adviser of King Louis XIII, was at the bottom of the trouble, and Rubens was advised to seek his favor by offering him a present in the form of a picture. The gift was well received, and the Cardinal, who followed the fashion of collecting works of art, commissioned two or three more pictures for himself. The finest of these is *The Flight of Lot*, a small picture, rich in color and full of expression and movement. Lot and his wife, assisted by guardian angels, are seen leaving their home slowly and unwillingly, in contrast to their two buxom daughters who follow them with the cheerful adventurousness of the young.

But having the Cardinal order pictures was one thing; getting him to confirm the enormous commission for the second gallery of the Luxembourg Palace was quite another. Richelieu continued to obstruct Rubens' appointment despite the painter's earlier understanding with the Queen Mother. Furthermore, there were even delays in payment for the work already done. Rubens, who had incurred considerable expense in transporting and setting up the pictures, let alone paying his expenses in Paris, was still waiting for any part of the 20,000 crowns that had been agreed upon as the price.

What had gone wrong? Rubens, in his heart, knew. Cardinal Richelieu had become aware that he was not merely a painter but a political agent of the Spanish Netherlands.

On his first visit to Paris in 1622 Rubens had done no more than carry friendly messages and gifts from Isabella to Marie. At that time Louis XIII was disposed to friendship with Spain and the Spanish Netherlands. But the situation altered when Cardinal Richelieu came into power. A man of keen political vision who worked unsparingly for the future greatness of the French monarchy, Richelieu regarded the Habsburgs, whether in Spain, Germany or the Netherlands, as a threat to France. He therefore set out to undermine their influence in Europe by every possible means. France was not yet strong enough to declare war, but the Cardinal evolved a policy of alliances with the principal Protestant powers, whom he subsidized to resist Habsburg Catholic aggression. By 1624 France had made treaties with the Kings of England and Denmark and with the Dutch Republic.

This coalition posed a serious threat to the Spanish Netherlands, and provided all the more reason for the Archduchess Isabella to attempt once again to end the war with the Dutch. During the summer of 1624 Rubens was in constant touch with his contacts in Holland for this purpose, and several times he discussed with Spinola the prospects for a truce. His relations with the Dutch may not have been known to Richelieu but his interviews with Spinola were certainly reported back to the Cardinal. Therefore, when Rubens returned to Paris in 1625 with the last Medici paintings, Richelieu was rightly suspicious of his intentions.

The Cardinal had more cause for concern when, at the time of Princess Henrietta's wedding, Rubens made personal contact with the Duke of Buckingham, the all-powerful favorite of England's King Charles I. The Duke, who was a connoisseur, a collector, and an admirer of Rubens, ordered a portrait of himself while he was in Paris. Rubens not only painted a magnificent equestrian portrait of the flamboyant Duke but also urged upon him the wisdom of a better understanding between England and the Spanish Netherlands. Buckingham was at the time bent on an aggressive war with Spain to increase England's power, but he was persuaded by Rubens at least to keep a back door open to negotiations. He agreed to remain in touch with Rubens, discreetly, under cover of buying pictures and antiques. He had in his employment a man of Flemish origin, a natural intriguer called Balthasar Gerbier who combined the careers of art dealer, miniature painter and spy. Gerbier was at the time concerned chiefly with finding pictures for Buckingham's collection, a function that enabled him to travel in the Netherlands and to keep in touch with Rubens without arousing too much suspicion.

Richelieu was probably aware of this arrangement, and it is therefore hardly surprising that he discouraged as far as he could the further employment of Rubens at the French court. He had no wish to expose his European system of alliances against Spain to this kind of insidious undermining. Hence the obstruction and delay of which Rubens complained; hence the difficulty in obtaining payment for the work he had already done. He was, in fact, eventually paid, but had it not been for the £500 that he received from Buckingham for his portrait, Rubens would hardly have been able to defray the immediate costs of his four-month sojourn in Paris.

On his return home in June 1625 Rubens heard joyful news. An important enemy fortress at Breda, near the Dutch border, had surrendered to Spinola after a long siege. The Archduchess went at once to visit her victorious army at the scene of the triumph. On her way back to Brussels she interrupted her journey at Antwerp to sit for a new portrait in honor of the occasion, and to hear what Rubens had to tell her of the political situation in France.

They also had another important matter to discuss. A few weeks before the surrender of Breda, Maurice, Prince of Orange, had died. For more than 30 years he had been the acknowledged leader of the Dutch in their struggle for independence, and his death was sure to have an effect on relations between the warring countries. Maurice's successor was his younger half-brother Frederick Henry, a man hitherto very little known in public affairs. He was eventually to prove himself a forceful leader, but in the first months after the death of Maurice and the fall of Breda, he thought it wise to play for time and to encourage the Archduchess to believe he would make a truce.

So once again Rubens was involved in cautious secret negotiations with his Dutch friends. But it was all to no purpose; the King of England, misled by Buckingham's dream of seizing control of the sea from Spain, concluded an alliance with the Dutch and sent the fleet to attack the Spanish port of Cadiz. The ill-planned venture was repulsed with heavy loss, while Rubens was left to bewail the collapse of his hopes. "When I consider the caprice . . . of Buckingham, I pity that young King who, through false counsel, is needlessly throwing himself and his kingdom into such an extremity. For anyone can start a war, when he wishes, but he cannot so easily end it."

Rubens' involvement in national affairs did not put a stop to his painting. In 1626 he was at work on another altarpiece for Antwerp's cathedral, where 12 years earlier he had painted the *Deposition* for the Arquebusiers' chapel. This time his commission was to decorate the high altar, and his subject was the Assumption of the Virgin. Remembering his disappointment as a young man when his altarpiece for the Chiesa Nuova in Rome could not be seen because of bad lighting, he insisted on painting the Antwerp altarpiece in the place for which it was intended, so that he could solve problems of visibility as they arose. The cathedral clergy willingly agreed, and for many months held their services in a side chapel while the high altar was curtained off to enable Rubens to work on the painting undisturbed.

While he was at work on the *Assumption,* Rubens' happy domestic life was shattered. Three years before, in 1623, his only daughter, Clara Serena, had died. She was 12 years old and, as he sadly wrote to his friend Peiresc, had already begun to reveal a most charming personality. An unfinished painting of a smiling little girl, with the bright eyes and tilted eyebrows of Isabella Rubens, is thought to represent Clara Serena *(page 18).* A year or two after his daughter's death, perhaps to cheer his wife, Rubens painted an amusing picture of his two boys *(page 19).* Albert, the elder, in black velvet with a hat, gloves and a book, is posed with his legs crossed in a consciously casual and grown-up attitude. He would be 11 or 12. Nicolas, four years younger, wears clear blue with yellow slashings, long stockings and stylish garters, and is intent on the pet finch that flutters from the perch he holds in his hand.

Then in the summer of 1626 Isabella Rubens died, after 17 years of happy marriage. It was a grievous blow. The cause of her death is unknown, and some have conjectured that she succumbed to the plague, which was prevalent that summer in Antwerp. Whatever the cause, Rubens found himself suddenly bereft of the beloved companion on whom his happy family life had so largely depended.

Rubens could not at first accept the loss with that resignation and self-control recommended by his favorite philosopher—Seneca. "I hope [time] will do for me what Reason ought to do," he wrote to his friend Pierre Dupuy in Paris; "for I have no pretensions about ever attaining a stoic equanimity; I do not believe that human feelings so closely in accord with their object are unbecoming to man's nature. . . . Truly I have lost an excellent companion, whom one could love—indeed had to love, with good reason—as having none of the faults of her sex. She had no capricious moods, no feminine weakness, but was all goodness and honesty. Because of her virtues she was loved during her lifetime, and mourned by all at her death. . . . I find it very hard to separate grief for this loss from the memory of a person whom I must love and cherish as long as I live. I should think a journey would be advisable, to take me away from the many things that necessarily renew my sorrow."

No immediate journey was in prospect, however, and he had to find comfort in his work and his religion. In the quietude of the cathedral he completed the great *Assumption* that still hangs there. The Virgin rises serenely into the heavens, supported by a summer cloud of cherubs, and is received by angels. The earthbound mourners gaze upward or look in wonder at the roses springing up in the empty tomb. The figure of the Virgin is suffused with the radiance of the skies, the eternal light that shines forever on those beyond the grave.

MUSÉE DU LOUVRE, PARIS

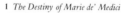

1 *The Destiny of Marie de' Medici* 21 *The Triumph of Truth*

A Queen Ennobled

In 1621 Rubens received his most important commission, a work which established his reputation internationally. The Dowager Queen of France, Marie de' Medici, widow of Henry IV, ordered a series of paintings to adorn the sumptuous residence that she was building in Paris, the Luxembourg Palace. The first 21 canvases that Rubens agreed to deliver were to depict the life of Marie herself—a subject close to the Queen's heart.

Rubens' task was not an easy one. Marie was no beauty, and her life had been relatively unglamorous; moreover, her marital relations had been marked by incessant quarreling, she had squandered huge sums of money and she had so antagonized her son, Louis XIII, that he once banished her from France. Rubens' flair for diplomacy must have been useful in his long discussions with the Queen about the paintings (he also submitted alternative subjects, and sketches for Marie's approval). Eventually, he solved his artistic problems and salved the Queen's vanity by clothing truth in allegory and by surrounding the lady *(right)* with handsome Greek gods and goddesses. For example, the first painting in the series *(above, left)* depicts the three Fates spinning the thread of life for the yet unborn Marie while Jupiter and Juno watch over them. In the final scene *(number 21, next to it)* Time, the healer, raises Truth to a meeting between the Queen and her son. In less than three years, Rubens completed the series, a Baroque masterpiece.

Clad in a rich robe embroidered with royal fleurs-de-lis, Marie de' Medici rides off from a symbolic victory on a spirited horse. While providing a fair likeness of his patron, Rubens tactfully smoothed her pudgy face and wrinkled neck.

Detail from *The Capture of Juliers (page 116, number 13)*

2 *The Birth of Marie de' Medici.* The goddess Juno presents the glowing figure of the infant Princess to a young woman who personifies the city of Florence, home of the Medici.

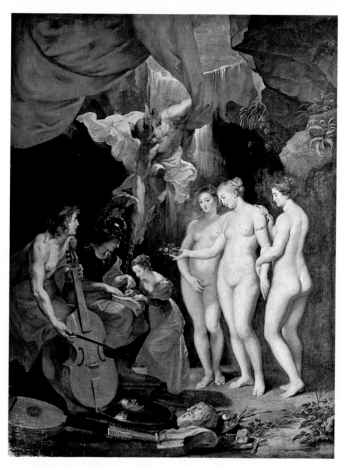

3 *The Education of Marie.* Minerva, Apollo and Mercury instruct Marie in the arts of music, reading and eloquence, while the nude figures of the Three Graces offer her beauty.

6 *Marie Arrives at Marseilles.* The helmeted figure of France welcomes Queen Marie while the goddess of Fame *(top)*, with heraldic trumpets, announces her arrival to the people.

7 *The Meeting at Lyons.* In 1600 Marie and Henry, already husband and wife, meet for the first time at Lyons, represented by the woman in the chariot drawn by two lions.

110

4 *The Presentation of the Portrait.* A portrait of Marie is shown to her future husband, King Henry IV, by two winged emissaries of Juno, the goddess of Marriage, who sits above.

5 *The Marriage by Proxy.* The Grand Duke of Tuscany, standing in for Henry IV—who was too busy to travel to Florence for his own marriage—places the wedding ring on Marie's finger.

8 *The Birth of Louis XIII.* The Queen gazes at her newborn son, who is held by the serpent-carrying figure of Health, while Fecundity offers her a basket of flowers and babies.

9 *Marie Becomes Regent.* Before setting out to war against Austria, Henry leaves his young son and France, symbolized by an orb marked with a fleur-de-lis, in Marie's care.

To cast Marie's past in the most favorable light, Rubens allegorically presented the Queen amid the gods of Olympus, flanked by water nymphs and cupids, fates and virtues. This device not only ennobled Marie's character but also allowed the artist to contrast elaborately robed French courtiers with a pantheon of nude gods and demigods, which he loved to paint. Populating his scenes are opulent and sensuous figures like the three brilliantly rendered naiads in the detail at left, who match their classic beauty with the elegance of the ladies of the 17th Century court.

Upon finishing the Medici series—he delivered the last paintings to Paris in February of 1625—Rubens had hoped to begin immediately on the canvases for the second gallery at the Luxembourg Palace. These paintings were to depict the life of Henry IV, a handsome, dynamic character who interested Rubens far more than the Queen. But Rubens never got beyond a few oil sketches and partly completed scenes. The powerful Cardinal Richelieu, chief adviser to Henry's son Louis XIII, was determined to prevent an alliance between France and Spain and, aware of Rubens' Spanish sympathies, he could not risk the artist's staying at Louis' court. The project was delayed again and again until finally Rubens abandoned hope of completing it. The finished Marie de' Medici paintings, however, became one of France's great treasures and one of Rubens' most enduring triumphs.

Detail from *Marie Arrives at Marseilles* (*page 110, number 6*)

10 *The Coronation of Marie.* To increase her power, Marie demanded that Henry allow her a separate coronation. Rubens' depiction of this event *(detail, right)* brilliantly captures the splendor of the French court.

11 *The Apotheosis of Henry IV.* The body of Henry, who was assassinated in Paris by a mad assailant, is carried aloft by Olympian figures *(left)* while the bereaved Marie *(right)* accepts the orb of government from France.

12 *Marie's Government.* To depict Marie's reign as sole ruler of France, Rubens portrayed her conferring with Jupiter *(top, left)* at a council of the gods. Apollo *(foreground, with bow)* is driving away her enemies.

Detail from *The Coronation of Marie*

13 *The Capture of Juliers.* Plumed and victorious after the fall of a disputed city, Marie is portrayed astride a white charger to show that, like her late husband, she was able to conquer enemies in battle.

14 *An Exchange of Princesses.* Anna of Spain *(left)* and Elizabeth of France *(right)* meet prior to their politically motivated double marriage—arranged by Marie—to each other's brother.

17 *The Queen Flees France.* Marie selected this subject to portray the heroic suffering she claimed to have endured when her son banished her for trying to rule in his place.

18 *An Offer of Negotiation.* Graciously accepting the olive branch from Mercury, while two of her ministers look on, Marie agrees to enter into talks with her son about her opposition to his government.

15 *Protector of the Arts.* Surrounded by Olympian gods and cupids holding pipes of Pan, paintbrushes and books, Marie presides over her nation's creative endeavors.

16 *The Majority of Louis XIII.* Having come of age, Louis takes over the tiller of the ship of state from the Queen Mother. The rowers are Strength, Faith, Justice and Prudence.

19 *Marie Consents to Peace.* Accepting peace with Louis, Marie is led by Mercury *(left)* into the Temple of Concord. The demons at right represent her enemies in France.

20 *The Reconciliation of Louis and Marie.* Louis is pictured as a young and handsome god, lifting his mother from the torment of her exile, symbolized by the Hydra-headed monster. *(See detail overleaf.)*

117

VI

In Quest
of Peace

Six months after his wife's death, Rubens decided to sell most of his collection of antiques, gems, coins and statues. He did not need the money, and so it has been generally assumed that the transaction had a political motive: the buyer was the Duke of Buckingham and the sale made a plausible excuse for Rubens to renew his connection with England's influential minister. Once again the Duke's agent was Balthasar Gerbier, who had come to the Netherlands ostensibly to arrange the sale.

Yet Rubens' motive may not have been entirely political. Certainly he could have found other excuses to see the Duke without sacrificing his treasured collection. Rubens' decision may also have had something to do with his wife's death. An active, extroverted man, he would find no comfort in lonely contemplation of the possessions he and Isabella had enjoyed together. As he had said himself in his letter to Pierre Dupuy, he needed a change of surroundings and ideas. During the next few years he was to become ever more deeply absorbed in political activities that took him away from home.

His painting was not neglected. The four years from 1626 to 1630, which marked the high point of his diplomatic activity, were only a partial interruption of his "beloved profession"—*la mia dolcissima professione*, as he called it. Though he naturally painted less than in the busy decades before, they were not unproductive years. He continued work on a number of commissions, and in the course of his travels he went through what almost amounted to a new training period—a time of gestation before the astounding fertility of his last years.

As soon as Rubens had completed the sale of his collection and had resumed contact with Buckingham through Gerbier, he began to explore the possibility of a peace between England and Spain. He acted of course with the full cognizance of the Archduchess and General Spinola, though they could not officially approve of any treaty while the King of Spain was still strongly opposed to peace with England. The necessity for peace was less apparent to Philip IV in Madrid than to the leaders of the Spanish Netherlands. In spite of Spinola's victories by land, the fact remained that the Dutch controlled the sea. Their ships blockaded the coast, intercepted convoys of arms and money from Spain and strangled the trade of Antwerp.

Rubens could observe every day as he walked or rode through the town the signs of growing distress: deserted streets, an empty harbor, workmen standing idle. "Our city goes step by step to ruin," he wrote to Dupuy in Paris. "It lives only upon its last reserve; there is no trade left to support it." The only hope for a return of prosperity lay in a truce with the Dutch that would end the blockade. Rubens hoped much of the English. They had a long tradition of alliance with the Dutch in the war against Spain; he believed that if England made peace with Spain, English influence would then be exerted on the Dutch Republic to bring the war in the Netherlands to an end. Rubens realized that any overture for peace would have to come from the English court because it was clear that with the present mood of Madrid no approach was to be expected from Spain. This, then, was the ultimate purpose of his renewed approach to Buckingham.

In the summer of 1627 he procured a passport to Holland on the grounds that unauthorized engravings of his work were in circulation there and he must take steps to defend his copyright. His real motive was to see Gerbier and communicate surreptitiously with his old friend Dudley Carleton, the English ambassador in The Hague. But on the subject of peace, the English proved no less obstinate than the Spanish. Neither Gerbier nor Carleton would discuss terms until Rubens put forward concrete suggestions for a cessation of arms—and that he had not been empowered to do.

So Rubens' first diplomatic mission of these years failed, but the trip was not a total loss: while in Holland he made a tour of the best-known studios. He went first to Utrecht, at that time the center of an important school of painters, most of whom had studied in Italy and whose works, strongly influenced by Caravaggio, had become very popular in the North. The painters of Utrecht received Rubens with the honors due to his immense reputation, and offered him a banquet. He spent some time in the studio of Gerrit van Honthorst, the most successful member of the group, and there he picked out for special commendation the work of a young German pupil, Sandrart.

The young man thus honored was instructed by Honthorst to act as a guide to Rubens during the rest of his short stay in Holland, a most fortunate circumstance for posterity, since Sandrart made notes of his impressions for later publication. Rubens talked freely, sharing with his young companion the fruits of his long experience and giving him many practical hints about his craft. "He was expeditious and industrious in his work," wrote Sandrart, "courteous and friendly to everyone, received with pleasure and beloved wherever he went." Rather more critically, he added that the great man was *said* to be very careful with his money, although he did spend generously on works of art. Sandrart also recorded Rubens' opinions of some of his contemporaries at home and abroad. Rubens told him, for instance, that he did not like the technique of Caravaggio, finding it too slow and heavy. Among Dutch painters he admired the work of Hendrick Terbrugghen of Utrecht, and particularly that of Frans Hals, the exuberant, feckless, brilliant portrait painter of Haarlem, who was one of Rubens' most sincere admirers. The traveler visited Terbrugghen and Hals as well as several artists in Amsterdam; but he knew nothing of another admirer, a young man of 21 called Rembrandt van Rijn, who had recently set up a studio in Leiden. Rembrandt would later in life possess that strange wild seascape, *Hero and Leander,* that Rubens had painted in Italy. But they were never to meet.

After his return to Antwerp, Rubens soon met again his admired young friend Anthony van Dyck, who in the summer of 1627 came back from Italy and took a house in Antwerp. He had traveled much in Italy, working in Genoa, Rome and Palermo, and had established his reputation as a portrait painter. His portraits, especially those that he had painted of the Genoese nobility, owed something to the portraits that Rubens had done there 20 years earlier. Van Dyck's equestrian picture of a young Italian nobleman has the subject riding forward toward the spectator in a composition frankly imitative of the portrait of the Duke of Lerma with which Rubens had so much impressed his contemporaries when he was van Dyck's age. But van Dyck substituted for the solid dignity of Rubens' treatment an airy elegance, which better suited the character of the young patrician.

Like Rubens, van Dyck was a man of striking appearance and accomplishments, but he was more openly ostentatious and less tactful and often did not get on well with other painters. He was fair, graceful, lively, always well and expensively dressed; he wore a sword and gave himself aristocratic airs which had earned him in Rome the nickname of *il pittore cavalleresco,* or, roughly, "the painter who acts like a fancy gentleman"—a name whose connotations were distinctly unflattering.

His house in Antwerp and the collection of antiquities and of fine pictures he had brought back from Italy attracted distinguished foreign visitors, as did the house and collection of Rubens. On at least one occasion Rubens made use of van Dyck's studio to contrive an unofficial meeting with a visiting English diplomat to drop hints about the renewal of negotiations for peace.

King Charles of England showed no sign of responding to such suggestions, and continued his belligerent attitude toward Spain. But Rubens was nevertheless appreciative of his growing stature as a collector and patron of the arts. It was some years now since Rubens had sent his *Lion Hunt* to Charles while he was still the Prince of Wales. A little later Charles had paid the artist the unusual compliment of asking him for a self-portrait. Rubens had first passed over the request, thinking it a mere whim and hesitating to send his own likeness to a prince. But when Charles had repeated the request he painted a suitably courtier-like portrait of himself, three-quarter face, in black, wearing a large black hat at a fashionable angle. It hangs to this day in the royal collection at Windsor Castle, a dignified and attractive picture, though not perhaps a very revealing one.

King Charles's reputation as art patron was enhanced in 1627 when he acquired the bulk of the Duke of Mantua's pictures. Vincenzo II of Mantua had continued the profligate ways of his father and through extravagance and a series of misfortunes and political errors had brought financial ruin to the family and forced the sale of its possessions. Rubens of course was very interested in the transaction; he had spent his most impressionable years among those great works of art and he owed his early opportunities and an important part of his development to the patronage of the Duke's father, Vincenzo I. As the cases of pictures trundled in wagonloads across Europe on their way to England, Rubens could only lament the despoiling of the palaces he had known and loved. But later he was thankful that the pictures had been moved before a worse fate befell them. The death of the childless Vincenzo II not long after the sale of his collection in 1627 precipitated a war over the succession, during which Mantua was sacked and looted by the French.

By early 1628 the court of Madrid was beginning to change its warlike attitude toward England. A year before, King Philip IV and his favorite, Gaspar de Guzman, Count of Olivares, had signed an ill-advised pact with France against England. A Protestant revolt in France had assumed serious proportions and Richelieu decided to make a temporary peace with the Habsburgs while he handled his domestic problems. Now Philip and Olivares were justifiably feeling doubtful of Richelieu's good faith, and were regretting the alliance. They summoned Spinola from Brussels for consultation, and on his advice seriously considered the question of peace with England.

In the summer of 1628, almost exactly a year after his abortive talks with Gerbier in Holland, Rubens, as the acknowledged expert on the English negotiations, was summoned to Madrid for what was to prove to be the most significant mission of his diplomatic career. Hurriedly he made legal provision for his two sons, appointing their grandfather Jan Brant and uncle Hendrik Brant as their guardians. Then he set off, traveling fast and secretly through France and reaching Madrid after a two-week journey. In Madrid he expounded his views, first to Olivares in several private audiences and then to the King in council. The Spanish court had never been known for quick decisions and Rubens' arrival coincided with news that caused even more hesitation than usual. The Duke of Buckingham, on whom all English policy depended and whom Rubens had been assiduously softening up for the past year, had been assassinated. How much was his removal likely to alter England's relations with Spain? Only time would show.

Then a few weeks later came the news that the Protestant stronghold of La Rochelle had at last capitulated; the Huguenot revolt in France was at an end, and Richelieu, free from trouble at home, had no further need of the alliance he had negotiated with Spain in 1627.

This made it all the more important for Spain to press for a peace treaty with England, but Philip's councilors continued to make delays and obstructions. Rubens asserted in a letter to a friend that "the difficulties are much more insoluble in words than in reality"; the Spanish court was infested with corrupt ministers, and the young King was dominated by his advisers. Rubens was exasperated by the situation. As he wrote to his friend Gevaerts in Antwerp: "The King alone arouses my sympathy. He is endowed by nature with all the gifts of body and spirit,

In pursuing his painting and diplomatic careers, Rubens became the best-traveled artist of his day, spending time in the cities indicated on this map. He left Antwerp in 1600 for an eight-year sojourn in Italy, which he interrupted with a trip to Spain for the Duke of Mantua. After returning to Antwerp, Rubens became a court painter. He made three trips to Paris while producing pictures for Marie de' Medici; in 1627 he spent several weeks touring the studios of Dutch artists and conducting diplomatic business for his country. His last journey was a 19-month mission to Madrid and London working for peace between Spain and England. On his way, he stopped in La Rochelle, France, to inspect the Huguenot fortification there, and in Cambridge, England, to receive an honorary degree. Rubens spent his last 10 years at home.

for in my daily intercourse with him I have learned to know him thoroughly. And he would surely be capable of governing under any conditions, were it not that he mistrusts himself and defers too much to others."

More than six months passed before Olivares and the King's council finally decided to employ Rubens on a peace mission to England. But Rubens spent the time profitably despite his anxiety and frustration. "Here I keep to painting, as I do everywhere," he wrote to Peiresc in Paris. He painted portraits of all the royal family for the Archduchess Isabella, who had never seen the King, her nephew *(page 20)*, or any of the younger generation of her Spanish family. For his own especial pleasure and interest Rubens studied once again the works in the royal collection, the great masterpieces of Titian, Tintoretto and Veronese.

On his previous visit to Spain in 1603, Rubens had gained a poor opinion of Spanish painters. He did not like their technique and thought most of their work coarse and lazy. On this second visit he met the young Sevillian, Velázquez, who had recently become Philip's court painter. He was the same age as van Dyck, a generation younger than Rubens, and he behaved with suitable respect toward the man who by this time had become acknowledged as the greatest master in Europe. If we believe the very plausible story told by Francisco Pacheco, historian of Spanish painting and father-in-law of Velázquez, Rubens recognized his merit instantly. Velázquez, so Pacheco asserts, accompanied Rubens on a tour of the Escorial and discussed the works of ancient and modern masters. Rubens, impressed by the young man's talent, urged the King to send him to Italy for a time to cultivate his genius and expand his knowledge. This advice, which was duly taken, marked an important stage in the development of Velázquez. Thus significantly did the paths of the two great painters intersect.

At last in April 1629 the long hesitation of Olivares came to an end and Rubens was authorized to proceed to England with overtures of peace. There was some doubt at the Spanish court as to the suitability of employing a professional painter for a diplomatic mission. In the rigid and complex social system of Europe, Rubens, the son of a lawyer, ranked as a gentleman; but a monarch as eminent as the King of Spain could be officially represented only by a nobleman. The King solved the problem by arranging that when he went to England Rubens should officially represent the Archduchess of the Spanish Netherlands rather than the King of Spain, and that he should be given the honorific title of Secretary to the Royal Council. This title, it was felt, would make up for the awkward fact that by profession he worked with his hands. Rubens accepted his new status with pleasure. Being nominated Secretary to the Royal Council would not add an inch to his stature as a painter or to his own estimate of himself, but he frankly enjoyed worldly honors.

Rubens hastened from Madrid to Brussels for a final briefing from the Archduchess, quickly visited his children and his studio in Antwerp, and then set sail, full of hope and expectation, for England.

The monarch with whom Rubens had come to plead for peace was by nature shy and fastidious, inhibited by an awkward stammer, lacking in natural ease, and not easy to know. Charles's great virtue was his genuine respect for men of genius. Together with the passport he had sent Rubens, he included a special message expressing his keen desire to become acquainted "with a person of such merit." This, from King Charles, was an unheard-of condescension. Nor was he disappointed when the painter was admitted to his presence. Rubens pleased him at once with his dignified manners and intelligent conversation. If the success of the negotiations had depended solely on an understanding between the King and the painter, all difficulties would have been quickly smoothed away.

But it was not to be quite so easy as that. Two serious obstacles had to be surmounted. In the first place Charles had an alliance with the Dutch and had agreed to make no peace with Spain without their consent. In the second place, his only sister was married to that unfortunate German Prince, Frederick V, who had allowed himself to be made the figurehead of the Protestant revolt in Bohemia that had triggered the Thirty Years' War. Since his defeat in Bohemia he had found refuge in Holland with his family, and the Dutch had taken up his cause. If King Charles made peace with Madrid he would certainly be accused by the Dutch and by his own Puritan subjects of betraying the interests of his Protestant brother-in-law in favor of Roman Catholic Spain.

Rubens understood these difficulties but was quick to grasp the all-important fact that the King had no personal sympathy with the Dutch. Charles believed in monarchy as divinely appointed. In his heart he regarded the republican Dutch as rebels against their lawful King. Soon he acknowledged to Rubens that if the Dutch refused to acknowledge the sovereignty of Spain on reasonable terms he would regard himself as absolved from all further obligation to them. Indeed he made so little secret of his growing hostility to them that he received the news of a recent Dutch victory in the Netherlands with tears in his eyes.

As to the lost cause of his unfortunate brother-in-law, he had at first insisted to Rubens that he would not make peace with Spain unless Frederick's lands in the Rhineland were restored. But his demands grew less vehement at every interview, and within a few weeks he conceded that he would be satisfied if the treaty with Spain included a face-saving clause of some kind about his brother-in-law's rights.

The hardest task Rubens had to face in England was that of outwitting the hostile ambassadors of France, Holland and Venice, all anxious to prevent a reconciliation between England and Spain. All of them worked openly or surreptitiously to throw obstacles in his way, either personally or through supporters in the court. "As to conditions in this Court," Rubens reported to Olivares, ". . . the first thing to be noted is the fact that all the leading nobles live on a sumptuous scale and spend money lavishly, so that the majority of them are hopelessly in debt. . . . That is why public and private interests are sold here for ready money. And I know from reliable sources that Cardinal Richelieu is very liberal and most experienced in gaining partisans in this manner." Thus Rubens' most dangerous and persistent foe was the French ambassador. But although he was supported by Queen Henrietta Maria and by a well-bribed court faction, the Frenchman's overbearing manner annoyed the King and contrasted unfavorably with Rubens' courtesy and restraint.

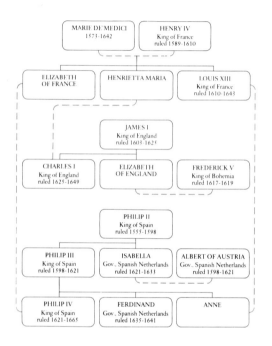

At the height of Rubens' diplomatic career, about 1630, the three dominant European kingdoms were intricately related by marriage (dotted lines). Each child of Marie de' Medici and Henry IV wore a crown: Louis as King of France, Elizabeth as wife to Spain's Philip IV, Henrietta Maria as the queen of Charles I of England. Thus, the three monarchs were brothers-in-law— Philip and Louis twice over since each married the other's sister.

Despite the vigilance his diplomatic mission demanded, Rubens found time to look about him and to enjoy the pleasures that England had to offer. He wrote with unaffected delight to Dupuy in Paris: "I feel consoled and rewarded by the mere pleasure in the fine sights I have seen on my travels. This island, for example, seems to me to be a spectacle worthy of the interest of every gentleman, not only for the beauty of the countryside and the charm of the nation; not only for the splendor of the outward culture, which seems to be extreme, as of a people rich and happy in the lap of peace, but also for the incredible quantity of excellent pictures, statues, and ancient inscriptions that are to be found in this Court."

The manners of the English also came as a pleasant surprise to him. "I find none of the crudeness that one might expect from a place so remote from Italian elegance," he wrote to Peiresc. The intellectual level was also high, and he found himself discussing points of Classical learning and archeological interest with such scholars as Sir Robert Cotton and Sir William Boswell. He called on the famous Swiss doctor, Sir Theodore Mayerne, who had settled in England, and discussed with him the qualities and composition of oil varnishes. He exchanged a few words in the street with Cornelius Drebbel, an inventor of some repute, who claimed among other things to have invented a ship that sailed under water. He visited Cambridge and received an honorary M.A. from that discriminating university.

His only regret among all these pleasures was that he sometimes felt too old to take in so many new impressions. He wrote with a touch of sadness to Dupuy: "To see so many varied countries and courts, in so short a time, would have been more fitting and useful to me in my youth than at my present age. My body would have been stronger to endure the hardships of travel, and my mind would have been able to prepare itself, by experience and familiarity with the most diverse peoples, for greater things in the future. Now, however, I am expending my declining strength, and no time remains to enjoy the fruits of so many labors."

This letter must have been written in one of his rare moods of despondency. But it is not surprising that this man of 52, who had been for many years at the head of his profession, should experience a shock on seeing again, in all their inspiring splendor, the transplanted masterpieces from the Mantua collection that had formed his style and his taste when he was young. The greater complexity of impressions received in maturity produces at first a sense of confusion, unlike the simple and direct impact that the mind absorbs in youth. But when he got back to Antwerp Rubens would find that despite his gloomy doubts, his experience abroad had indeed fitted him "for greater things in the future."

Rubens was staying in the London house of his old friend Gerbier, and, having been starved for family life over a long period, he took much delight in Gerbier's numerous children. He also was able to set up a temporary studio there and spend some time at his easel. He painted a sumptuous allegory, *The Blessings of Peace*, as a present for the King, a very suitable subject in view of his mission. He also painted another picture, *Landscape with St. George*, apparently for his own pleasure and as a symbolic record of his visit. The setting is based on the Thames landscape and represents an open valley with a winding river. The conflict is already over—the dragon lies slain and St. George, a young knight who is evidently King Charles I, tenderly greets the smiling princess. She is, in the Rubens manner, rather more plump and blonde than Charles's Queen, Henrietta Maria, but could be taken for her with the exercise of a little imagination. This pleasing fantasy was bought from Rubens a year or two later by an English connoisseur who gave it to the King and Queen. It is still in the royal collection.

The most exciting event for Rubens the artist during his stay in England was his receipt, at long last, of the commission to decorate the ceiling of the King's great Banqueting House in Whitehall. It had been eight years since the first hint of this commission was dropped, and now hope became reality. The noble building by Inigo Jones was almost complete. Its immense ceiling was divided into nine partitions, which gave scope for a scheme of pictures comparable to the gorgeous compositions of Tintoretto and Veronese that Rubens had admired in Venice.

The King wished the nine pictures to represent the blessings of his father's reign. The subject presented no difficulties to Rubens, who had, after all, contrived to invent 21 pictures to celebrate the inglorious life of Marie de' Medici. The late King James had not been a great king, but he had worked sincerely for the peace and prosperity of his people and had been moderately successful in his aim; the subject had great possibilities. A sum of £3,000 was agreed upon as the price, and Rubens was to begin on the work as soon as he got back to Antwerp.

Rubens' pleasure over the Whitehall commission was soon crowned by the success of his diplomatic mission: Charles decided to make peace. After months of vacillation, the King recognized the hard facts: the state of his finances made further war with Spain a luxury he could not afford. Rubens was instructed to stay in London until the Spanish ambassador arrived to draw up a treaty; owing to the usual delays at Madrid, that event did not occur until the following February.

The interim cost Rubens some anxiety. First of all, he could not forget his dream of a peacefully reunited Netherlands. Elated by his success in negotiating peace between England and Spain, he was convinced that the Dutch, weakened by the desertion of the English, would now at last make peace too. He resolved to make an independent approach to their ambassador in London, the venerable career diplomat Albert Joachimi. Rubens pointed out to him that it would be advisable for the Dutch to conclude their rebellion against Spain on any reasonable terms. By "reasonable terms" Rubens meant that they should accept the sovereignty of Spain, while receiving substantial guarantees of self-government.

Joachimi replied tersely that the Netherlands could be reunited only if North and South joined together to expel the Spaniard. The answer startled and embarrassed Rubens. He had two deep and abiding loyalties —to the Catholic Church and the Crown of Spain. He seems not to have realized, until he came face to face with Joachimi, that both these loyalties were anathema to the majority of the Dutch. His own political contacts had always been with the waverers, with Catholics and Catholic sympathizers, and he had made the not uncommon mistake of believing that the views of his personal friends were much more widespread than they really were. Joachimi pursued his advantage by saying that a reunion of the Netherlands would only be possible on the terms of the so-called Pacification of Ghent. This Pacification had taken place a year before Rubens was born; it marked the brief epoch in the Dutch war of independence when the Southern Netherlands, exasperated by the indiscipline of the Spanish troops, had made common cause with the North to expel them. To a loyal subject of the Spanish Netherlands like Rubens, the Pacification of Ghent had been a temporary and deplorable deviation from the path of loyalty, legality and obedience. Better a war, said Rubens, than a revival of that dishonorable pact.

The rebuff distressed Rubens and brought him a moment of painful awakening. Now at last he saw that peace and reunion between the North and the South could not be obtained by fair words and persuasive arguments about ancient loyalties. The Dutch Republic had become a self-reliant, successful, independent state and would remain so.

Some time before this disheartening encounter with Joachimi, Rubens heard from Antwerp that his son Albert was ill, and for several weeks he was deeply troubled, until he had word from his friend Gevaerts of the boy's recovery. Furthermore, Rubens was worried about being so long away from his studio. "My domestic affairs . . . are going to ruin by my long absence," he complained in a letter to Olivares, "and can be restored to order only by my own presence." In a more intimate note to Gevaerts he said: "I should like to go home and remain there all my life."

In March 1630, after a year and seven months away in Spain and England, Rubens was at last free to go home. At his final audience with the King, Charles gave him the honor of knighthood, and presented him with the elegant sword with which he performed the ceremony. He also gave him a diamond ring from his own finger and a diamond hatband—costly and honorable gifts that reflected a genuine esteem and affection. Even the formal patent of knighthood was drawn up in terms of unusual warmth: "We grant him this title of nobility because of his attachment to our person and the services he has rendered to us and to our subjects, his rare devotion to his own sovereign and the skill with which he has worked to restore a good understanding between the crowns of England and Spain."

In every immediate sense Sir Peter Paul's mission to England had succeeded, and he set sail for Antwerp in the mild March weather full of happy anticipations for the future. At his departure he was able to do a good deed of a kind very much after his own heart. The Catholic minority in England, laboring under heavy penal laws, were forbidden to send their children abroad to school. They did so, nonetheless, by taking advantage of diplomatic immunity to find passage for the young people in ambassadorial ships. Rubens appears to have made his homeward journey with a bevy of boys and girls bound for Catholic schools on the continent.

And as he traveled, his hopes and ambitions happily centered on his long-neglected studio at Antwerp and the great pictures he was going to paint for the King of England.

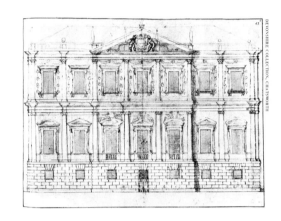

In 1629 Rubens was commissioned to provide ceiling paintings for the Royal Banqueting House in London, shown above in a preliminary design by the architect Inigo Jones. (In Jones's final scheme the triangular pediment and the central doorway were eliminated.) The ceiling plan below shows the nine panels that received Rubens' huge canvases (page 140). The ceiling measures 110 feet by 55 feet; the central oval is 32 feet long and 20 and a half feet wide.

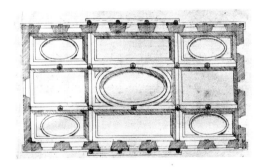

A Swift and Confident Hand

Rubens' genius lay in painting, but the grace and vitality of the hundreds of his drawings that still exist place him among the great draftsmen of all time. Many of his sketches, like the one at right, are chalk studies, which he made to work out a feature of a large painting or to show a patron how a finished work would look. Others, done in greater detail, are linear versions of his own paintings that he supplied to engravers to be made into prints. His drawings are based on an extraordinary variety of subjects from a great many sources. They include copies of the works of other artists from antiquity, the near past and his own age, sketches of his children and the landscape around him, which he made for pleasure or for possible future use in paintings. Whatever the subject, he invariably drew with the hand of a painter, softening outlines and building up shapes that seemed to take on life and color even in black and white.

Unlike many artists, who labored to produce technically perfect and minutely finished drawings, Rubens often sacrificed detail to gain a sense of movement and energy. He certainly felt that his drawings should be considered differently from his paintings as works of art; in any case, he never signed any of them. Drawing was not only basic to his profession but a source of enjoyment. In one of his paintings, when he wanted to illustrate Mars destroying a thing of beauty, he showed the war god trampling on a sketch.

A chalk sketch of a pensive girl illustrates how Rubens suggested substance and contour by soft, deep modeling of the face and hands. He drew this portrait from life and used it as a study for the figure of the Virgin in one of his paintings.

A Young Woman with Crossed Hands, c. 1630

A Young Woman with Ostrich Fan, 1632-1635

Before he started work on one of his paintings, Rubens often made drawings of the principal figures from models. The sketches shown here are costume studies for one of his most popular works, *The Garden of Love.* (Drawings that Rubens made for engravings of parts of the same painting appear as the end papers of this book.) The painting itself *(page 188)* shows an elegant gathering where couples flirt and talk in a garden; in spirit it is a recasting of a mythological feast in contemporary dress, an idea that was to be popularized in the 18th Century by the French painter Watteau and others.

Each of the figures in these sketches was changed in the final painting. Rubens rarely transferred a figure intact from chalk to paint; for him the purpose of many of the drawings seems to have been to explore subtle alternatives of pose, gesture and costume before beginning to paint. Later, when working on the painting, he would add the touches of color, shape and texture that brought each element and the scene itself to perfection.

A Young Woman Kneeling, c. 1632-1635

A Young Man Walking, c. 1632-1635

Portrait of a Little Boy (Nicolas Rubens), c. 1619

Rubens' children were among his favorite models, and he made many affectionate sketches of his son Nicolas like the two shown here. The artist used the portrait above as a model for the Infant Christ in one of his paintings; other portraits of Nicolas and of his older brother Albert appear repeatedly in Rubens' works as cherubs. Like some of his drawings, the one above bears the inscription "P. P. Rubbens" in the lower right corner.

Portrait Study of Nicolas, 1625-1626

However, it is not the artist's signature; it was added by another hand, possibly that of a collector who wanted to identify his possession and enhance its value.

Realizing how valuable his drawings would be to a serious artist, Rubens left them in his will to any of his sons or sons-in-law who might wish to take up a career as a painter. But none of them did, and the sketches, unfortunately, were sold and scattered.

Study for the Figure of Christ on the Cross, c. 1614-1615

Although Rubens is probably best known as a painter of the female nude, in his drawings the male nude occurs with greater frequency. Long practice in painting his ideal vision of the female figure evidently enabled him to transfer it from his mind to the canvas directly and spontaneously. But apparently he did not feel as confident about depicting men, and he made many study sketches like the ones on these pages. All three of these were made for paintings that depicted Christ's crucifixion. The two men on this page appear straining to lift the Cross; the haunting figure opposite is a study for the crucified Christ.

Like his female figures, Rubens' males have an almost superhuman quality; their twisting torsos and bulging muscles represent an idealization of the body. It may have been to help achieve this effect that the artist drew many of his male figures not only from life, but from Classical sculptures and the mighty marble giants of Michelangelo.

A Man Holding the Shaft of the Cross, c. 1601

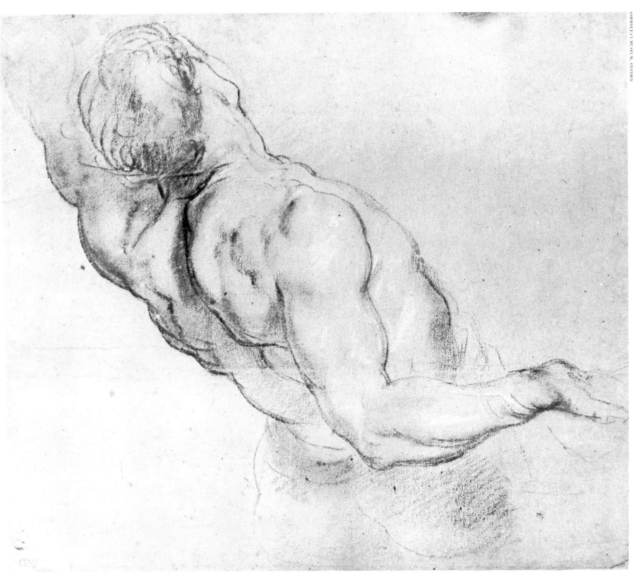

Study of a Nude Male Torso, c. 1610-1611

137

Rubens rarely painted landscapes—the demand for his work kept him busy on action scenes—but he did make many sketches of his beloved Flemish countryside. He may have used some of these as studies for the backgrounds of paintings (like other artists of his day, he did not take his easel outside to paint directly from nature). However, he often hired associates like Jan Brueghel or Jan Wildens to fill in the landscapes in his paintings. It is more likely that when he rode in the country for relaxation, he stopped to sketch when he saw a gate or bridge, or even a cluster of brambles (below) that he found particularly pleasing.

Brambles, c. 1615-1

Woodland Scene, c. 1635-1638

A Country Lane, 1615-1618

VII

Youth Renewed

On his return to Antwerp from England in 1630 Rubens immediately resumed his interrupted career. Soon his studio was fully occupied with large commissions: besides the nine canvases for the King of England's Banqueting House there was a new series of designs for tapestries depicting the life of Achilles, as well as the series representing the life of Henry IV, which Marie de' Medici, despite the opposition of Richelieu, was still determined to have.

Other difficulties besides politics bedeviled this ill-fated project. New measurements had come from the palace architect in Paris, quite different from those that had been sent before. Rubens complained that he would have to "mutilate, spoil, and change" almost all his designs, and he wrote in justifiable annoyance pleading for six inches more space "so that I need not cut off the head of the King seated on his triumphal chariot." Pending an answer, he suspended the work altogether. At the time he felt angry and frustrated, but nine months later, when Marie de' Medici quarreled finally with the all-powerful Richelieu and fled from France, he was thankful that he had spent no more time on a project that after almost 10 years of negotiations finally had to be abandoned.

Now that he was settled again in his own home, Rubens felt the need of a wife. Some of his friends had urged him to mark his elevation in the world by choosing a noblewoman. (A few years later Anthony van Dyck, in England, was to make a noble marriage to Mary Ruthven, a lady of the court descended from the Earls of Gowrie.) But, as Rubens confided in a letter to Peiresc, he feared the haughty temper of a court lady and decided to marry "a young wife from a respectable bourgeois family . . . who would not blush to see me take my brushes in hand." He made it all sound very sober and prudent, but he did not bother to mention to his old friend that the respectable bourgeois wife he had chosen was a dazzling beauty of 16.

There is something a little comic in Rubens' representation of his second marriage as a prudent measure. It was not thought prudent in the 17th Century, any more than it is today, for a widower of 53 to marry a girl of 16. But in this, as in so much else, Rubens was fortunate. Hélène

Fourment was the youngest daughter of his old friend and neighbor Daniel Fourment—and a niece of his first wife, Isabella. It was Hélène whom Rubens had probably used as a model when she was a pretty girl of 10, and it was her older sister, Susanna, who had posed for his portrait *Le Chapeau de Paille*.

The wedding took place on December 6, 1630. Gevaerts wrote a Latin poem in honor of the occasion in which he declared that Helen of Antwerp, unlike Helen of Troy, would be the perfect wife, in whose arms the greatest of painters would renew his youth. The prediction was just on both counts—Hélène was to be the happiness and inspiration of Rubens' last 10 years. Those autumnal words Rubens had written from England the year before, lamenting that it was too late for him to profit by new impressions, were disproved by the fertility and freshness of his invention in the decade that remained to him.

He painted Hélène many times. The first portrait, done probably at about the time of the marriage, shows her seated in a chair, leaning a little forward as though just about to spring out of it. She is very richly dressed; a sprig of flowers adorns her golden hair; her skin, the gleaming pearls in her ears and round her neck, her ribbons, brocade and lace are painted with consummate skill.

In that delightful double portrait that Rubens had painted to commemorate his first marriage 21 years earlier, he had given the same masterly attention to Isabella's delicate young face and to the elegant details of her fine clothes. But his portrait of Hélène is different in feeling. It is not wholly a matter of style, though style has much to do with it. His portrait of Isabella is a direct statement, firm in outline, precise in detail. The portrait of Hélène is in his later manner: shape and texture are conveyed by the interplay of tones; the whole surface shimmers with points of light; the effect is softer, and the contrasts between colors and light and shade are gentler than in his earlier work.

When he painted his wedding portrait with Isabella they were both young; he understood the gaiety and confidence of youth, but not its pathos. Now that he was old, he could see in this young girl, his wife, almost bouncing out of her chair with health and vitality, the transience of youth. He had painted Isabella as though the moment could be eternal and she would never cease to be that pretty, well-dressed bride sitting so demurely still. He painted Hélène leaning forward to meet and enjoy every moment of her life, as beautiful as a flower and as ephemeral.

Many other portraits followed: Hélène in a plumed hat; Hélène with an ostrich-feather fan; Hélène out walking. A gay and amusing picture shows Rubens and Hélène in the garden of their house. She is in a shady hat and light summer dress and has turned to speak to a boy in red, probably her stepson Nicolas. In the background is the Italianate pavilion with which Rubens had adorned his garden, a fountain, trees and an enclosure with tulips in bloom; in the foreground, in contrast to this formal setting, an old servant feeds a peacock, a turkey gobbles among its chickens and a dog dashes up.

Perhaps Rubens' most moving portrait of Hélène is an unfinished study of her with two of their children *(page 177)*. She must have been

21 or 22 by this time. She holds her little boy Frans on her knee, and her eldest child, Clara Johanna, leans toward her on one side. The unforced simplicity of the group suggests that Rubens got his first impression for it by coming upon his wife and children at some ordinary domestic moment when no thought of posing was in anyone's mind. Her face wears the grave, tender, absorbed expression of a young mother alone and happy with her children.

There is a strong popular belief that Hélène frequently posed for Rubens as a model for the many naked nymphs and goddesses that decorate his later paintings. The King of Spain was once confidentially informed that the naked Venus in a *Judgment of Paris* he had ordered was a portrait of the painter's wife, "who is without doubt the best-looking woman at present in this country." But actually there is no evidence that Rubens habitually used her as a model. If one starts looking for Hélène in Rubens' work one finds oneself recognizing her in pictures painted before he married her, or even before she was born. The truth of the matter probably lies in the fact that Rubens always had admired her type of beauty—fair, pink and white, abundantly healthy, and with those generous contours which give a peculiarly luminous quality to reflected light.

He did paint Hélène half-naked once, in her own character, and it is one of his best-known portraits *(page 164)*. She stands in an attitude that looks accidental, clutching a fur-lined coat round her as though she had been surprised while dressing. In capturing the contrast of texture between the silky fur of the coat and the silky skin of his wife, Rubens had in mind a famous picture by Titian of a girl in a fur coat that he had seen and copied while he was in England. But except for its technical skill, Rubens' version of Hélène has little in common with Titian's sensuous and deliberately titillating picture. Hélène makes no particular effort to show off her charms, but merely stands there with a hint of impatience in the set of her feet, as though she wished he would finish the picture and let her get on with her dressing. It is an intimate picture, a part of their private life; with affectionate accuracy, Rubens even painted her feet as they really were, the big toe crushed a little sideways by the wearing of tight shoes. He emphasized the personal character of the picture in his will by specifically leaving it to her—calling it *Het Pelsken —The Little Fur*. He did not wish this bedroom study, done for his own pleasure and Hélène's, to be put up for auction with his salable assets and handed about among strangers.

There is little doubt that the influence of this happy second marriage pervades much of his later work. Soon after the wedding, inspired in equal measure by a renewed study of Titian and his recapture of domestic happiness, he painted an ebullient Arcadian landscape *(pages 154-157)*. Dancing nymphs and satyrs embrace under the shade of trees, while young maidens make offerings to a statue of Venus, and the green grass and leafy branches are thronged with dozens of cupids playing, dancing and flying; it is a lyrical evocation of sensual happiness, illuminated by the varied color and mellow light of a country summer's day.

Somewhat later, in a picture called *The Garden of Love (pages 132, 133 and end papers)*, Rubens treated the happiness of lovers in a more contemporary manner. On a flowery lawn, against a parklike background with an Italian pavilion and fountain, a party of elegant young people stroll, sit and flirt. It is an open-air picture with the hazy, languorous atmosphere of a long summer evening, and the women in their different-colored silks are like flowers. Rubens may have been inspired by the fashionable love poems of the day—graceful, sensuous and witty—for he did not himself call his picture *The Garden of Love;* he called it *Conversation à la Mode*. Under whatever name it goes, it is surely Rubens' personal tribute to the gallantry and grace of his young wife's generation.

The idea of a garden given over to the happiness of young lovers goes back to medieval times and to the elaborate conventions of courtly love. French painters of the 16th Century had revived the idea in gaily erotic paintings that Rubens would have seen on his visits to Paris and Fontainebleau. He breathed a new life into the time-honored fantasy, which, through the influence of this picture, returned to France as a fashionable subject in the 18th Century. Antoine Watteau, fascinated by the art of Rubens, heightened the theme of lovers in a garden with a tender and subtle nostalgia of his own, but a host of later imitators reduced it at last to sentimental prettiness.

Meanwhile Rubens did not neglect more solemn subjects. The Archduchess Isabella had celebrated his return from England by commissioning an altarpiece in honor of the Spanish mystic, St. Ildefonso. The saint had been Bishop of Toledo in the Seventh Century, and Archduke Albert had established a fraternity of laymen in his honor in Brussels. The altarpiece was in the traditional Netherlandish form of a triptych. On the wings the Archduchess and her husband appeared kneeling in prayer, each under the protection of a patron saint. Rubens depicted Isabella and Albert in the prime of life, as they had been when they first came to the Netherlands, dignified representatives of a ruling caste reverently acknowledging the only power that was higher than their own.

On the triptych's central panel Rubens painted St. Ildefonso's vision of the Virgin, who had bestowed on him a shining vestment. The kneeling saint leans forward to embrace the folds of the sacred robe offered to him by a motherly and smiling Mary, enthroned between attendant female saints. Brilliant lighting conveys the golden radiance of a celestial vision. The ceremony, dignified but intimate, may be reminiscent of the court at Brussels where Rubens often must have seen the Archduchess, attended by her well-behaved maids of honor, graciously receiving some venerable prelate.

In his spare time Rubens was still drawing title pages for the Plantin press. These sometimes took the form of a pictorial commentary not unlike a modern publisher's "blurb," and provided opportunities for Rubens to demonstrate his ample knowledge of symbolism and emblems. Thus the compendious title page for the works of the classical scholar Hubert Goltzius shows at the top of the sheet a bust crowned with laurel and garlanded with a necklace of ancient coins to represent Antiquity. On the right, Time and Death overcome a group of warriors representing the Roman, Greek, Persian and Median Empires; on the left the god Mercury is seen digging up ancient statues while Hercules gathers smaller objects such as coins in a cornucopia, and the goddess Athena, holding the torch of enlightenment, stands ready to explain their meaning. The whole is surmounted by a phoenix, symbol of the rebirth of the long-buried past through the efforts of modern scholarship.

This overloaded page bears eloquent witness to the continued enthusiasm of Rubens for antiquarian studies, an enthusiasm shared by his son Albert, who was now studying Greek. When the boy had advanced enough, Rubens had him copy out obscure passages in Greek sources to illustrate a learned discussion he was carrying on by letter with Peiresc. He added suitably dutiful messages on the boy's behalf: "He honors your name above all, and reveres your noble genius." Whether Albert felt all he was said to feel about the learned Peiresc is open to doubt. A few years later, when Rubens sent him to Italy to complete his education, Albert made no attempt to visit his father's old friend on the way. But he proved, in the end, to be a reasonably good antiquarian in his own right, and something of an authority on Roman coinage.

Rubens had bought no more statues since he had sold his collection to the Duke of Buckingham, but he had kept a few of his gems and cameos and now he began to add to them again. In her first confinement Hélène took liquid food from an engraved antique porringer that was one of his special treasures. (Peiresc thought it was a modern fake, but was too courteous to say so to Rubens.)

His collection of pictures was also growing. He had made several more copies of Titian while in Spain and England. He also bought original works of his contemporaries. He owned four by his late friend Elsheimer and at least 10 by van Dyck, who, not long after the return of Rubens to Antwerp, went over to England as court painter to Charles I, a post he filled on and off for the next seven years.

Van Dyck had long since outgrown the influence of Rubens, though they appear always to have been on friendly terms; but another young painter of a very different character came into Rubens' life at some time in the 1630s. This was Adriaen Brouwer, who reached Antwerp by way of Haarlem, where he had been associated for a time with Frans Hals. He painted mostly small, sad landscapes, or pictures of drunken and joyless revelry among the poor. His best pictures have an intense Goya-like quality quite unlike the cheerful aura of the paintings of his more jovial compatriots. Brouwer lived a hard, short life; he was of a proud and independent spirit, restless but melancholic. According to tradition, Rubens found him in prison for debt, obtained his release, clothed and fed him and put him on his feet again—until his next drunken bout landed him in more trouble. But there is no real evidence of any such sequence of events, and research indicates that undercover political activity might have been the cause of his imprisonment. If he was a political agent he may well have had some right to help from Rubens. It is also possible that the fatal weakness which shortened his life was not drink, as generally assumed, but drugs. Hemp-smoking had recently gained a hold in the Netherlands and the figures with clay pipes in some of his small groups have the trancelike, obsessive stare of drug addicts. Whatever the dismal cause, Brouwer died at 32.

Whether or not some political connection existed between the two, Rubens admired Brouwer's work. He bought 17 of his pictures—more than he acquired by any other living painter. And his own work shows signs of Brouwer's influence, especially in the treatment of landscape. It was typical of Rubens' appetite for impressions and ideas that he could, in spite of his age and fame, acquire new skills by studying the work of a man 30 years his junior. It is an unexpected link, this one between Rubens, the uninhibited believer in the goodness of life, and Brouwer, with his claustrophobic vision of man's debasement.

Although Rubens had announced his intention of withdrawing from politics, the Archduchess continued to rely on him for advice. Then in the summer of 1631 she insisted on his undertaking a new and difficult mission. He could hardly refuse, since it concerned the Queen Mother of France, Marie de' Medici. Marie had found it impossible to stop meddling in politics, and had sought to regain her influence over her son Louis XIII by undermining the all-powerful Cardinal Richelieu. Her ill-managed intrigues ended in disaster and she had to flee for safety to the Netherlands. Rubens, who was asked to welcome her on behalf of the Archduchess, found her full of a plan for raising a rebellion at home to be led by her younger son, the Duke d'Orléans, and to be joined (as she confidently expected) by half the nobility in France. All she needed, she averred, was a little financial help from Spain, and her friends would quickly overthrow the Cardinal.

How much was the peace-loving Rubens truly in favor of this blood-thirsty scheme for precipitating civil war in France? He knew Marie de' Medici, her worthless younger son and her whole entourage well enough to distrust their skill and perseverance in any major undertaking. But Richelieu was, unquestionably, a dangerous enemy to Spain and the Spanish Netherlands, and any chance of bringing him down seemed worth exploiting. Accordingly, Rubens, in a lengthy dispatch, urged the court in Madrid to subsidize the projected rebellion; he wasted weeks visiting the intrigue-ridden household of the Queen Mother and escorting her through his studio and around the Plantin press when she made a state visit to Antwerp.

Not surprisingly, Marie's conspiracy came to naught, and in the spring of 1632 Rubens implored the Archduchess to release him from any further duties of this kind. "This favor I obtained with more difficulty than any other she ever granted me," he wrote. Even so, his release was incomplete. He was no longer required to take any part in the dubious plots of Marie de' Medici, but he was still to be employed on peace missions to the Prince of Orange.

The need for a truce with the Dutch was more urgent than ever. Financial help from Spain was becoming unreliable, and the land war was going badly for the Spanish Netherlands, with badly paid troops and a discontented populace. In August 1632, the Dutch took the border fortress of Maastricht and were in a position to threaten Brussels. That they did not advance on the capital was due not to any military skill on the part of the defenders, but to the halfheartedness of the invaders, who were now themselves beginning to wonder if a friendly buffer state be-

A French engraving of 1628 allegorically celebrates Cardinal Richelieu's energetic regime as the chief minister of Louis XIII. Richelieu is shown plucking from a fleur-de-lis the worm of heresy—probably a reference to a recent defeat of the Protestant Huguenot rebels. At his feet the thorns of rebellion lie harmless, an allusion to the vain attempt by a group of disgruntled noblemen to do away with the King and the Cardinal. The lion of Spain and an eagle representing the Habsburg Empire are shown chained, to indicate Richelieu's success in keeping those enemies of France temporarily in check.

tween the Dutch Republic and Richelieu's increasingly aggressive France to the south might not after all serve a useful purpose. A truce, or even real peace, with the Spanish Netherlands would be one way of achieving this desirable effect.

So in hope of a settlement with the Dutch, and out of loyalty to the aging Archduchess, Rubens agreed to continue his confidential negotiations. But the situation of his own country was now such that he laid himself open to grave misunderstanding from some of his countrymen. When he had discussed the future of the Netherlands with the Dutch Ambassador Joachimi in London he had been startled to realize that the Dutch would accept no peace with the South unless the South joined them in rejecting the sovereignty of Spain. While this had been unthinkable for a loyalist and Catholic like Rubens, it was not unthinkable for a growing number of his compatriots who, now that the war was going badly, had forgotten the earlier benefits conferred on their country by the benevolent rule of the Archduchess, and resented the unending conflict in the interests of Spain.

The malcontents did not realize that there was, unhappily for them, no preferable alternative. It was too late to re-establish the ancient confederation of the Netherlands as it had once been. If the South were to throw off the rule—and protection—of Spain, it would inevitably have to submit to the political and economic dominance of the North, which would be of no advantage to the Southerners' commerce and very wounding to their pride.

Nevertheless, the discontent of the people grew alarmingly, and in the autumn of 1632, the Archduchess convened the Estates General, the representative assembly of the Spanish Netherlands, for the first time in 32 years. The delegates insisted that overtures of peace be made, not privately to the Prince of Orange as Isabella had planned, but formally to the Dutch Estates. The Archduchess, who tended to believe, like many royal rulers, that matters of state could be settled on a personal basis, reluctantly authorized them to send an official deputation to The Hague, but commanded Rubens to go at the same time. The delegates were indignant, refused to believe her assertion that Rubens was empowered only to help and advise them, and suspected her (quite rightly) of having given him secret instructions.

The leader of the deputation was the haughty Duke of Aerschot, who had always disliked the prominence of Rubens at court, and he made it clear that he would not tolerate Rubens as an independent envoy. Stopping in Antwerp on his way to The Hague, he let it be known that he expected Rubens to report to him. Rubens, obeying the commands of the Archduchess, sent his excuses and did not do so. Aerschot exploded with rage: "I might well have omitted doing you the honor to reply," he wrote, "since you have not only failed in your duty by not calling on me in person, but even had the impertinence to write me a note, which could only be suitable between equals. . . . All that I can say is that I should be well content if you would learn, for the future, how people of your rank should behave to people of mine."

Aerschot sent a copy of his letter with undisguised glee to the Estates

A triumphal arch, richly emblazoned with allegorical and historical scenes, was one of many decorations built to Rubens' designs for the reception of a new governor of the Spanish Netherlands, the Cardinal Infant Ferdinand. The reception was the grandest in Antwerp's history; Ferdinand was so impressed that he refused a present of 9,000 florins offered him by the city and accepted instead several of the best paintings that Rubens had done as part of the decorations.

General. So public an insult naturally made it impossible for Rubens to take any further part in the negotiations—which were undertaken without him, and which proved as abortive in the hands of the official deputation as they had previously been in his own.

In some ways Aerschot's open insult may have helped restore Rubens' popularity with his compatriots. He had always acted with undeviating loyalty to the Archduchess, the legitimate ruler of the Spanish Netherlands, but the difficulty of the times had forced him, during the last few months, into a questionable position, and made him the target of much muttered criticism in the Estates General for putting the interests of Spain before those of his own country. When the Spanish government was unpopular, this was the obvious criticism to make of those who remained loyal to it. Yet for many years his fellow citizens had been justly proud of his fame and had looked to him with gratitude for bringing honor and distinction to his country and for resisting all temptations to leave Flanders for more profitable work elsewhere—in England, Spain, France or Italy. The Duke of Aerschot's offensive behavior to such a man embarrassed even the Duke's supporters and left Rubens with his popular reputation restored.

At the end of that year, 1633, the Archduchess died. She had been Rubens' patroness and friend for a quarter of a century. Within the formal framework that conditioned the relations of a royal ruler and a subject, theirs had been a real friendship, based on mutual understanding and respect, and Rubens mourned her sincerely. But her death gave him the opportunity once and for all to retreat into private life. It was as a painter and not as a political adviser that he welcomed her successor in the government of the Spanish Netherlands.

He was Ferdinand, 25-year-old younger brother of King Philip IV of Spain, and known to his contemporaries by the title of the Cardinal Infant. "Infant" was the term habitually used in Spain to designate a prince of the blood: Ferdinand was called "Cardinal" because he had originally been intended for the Church and in fact had been created a cardinal when he was little more than a boy (Rubens, on his visit to Madrid in 1628, had painted him as a rather shy-looking adolescent in cardinal robes). But the youthful cardinal had ambitions to be a soldier, which were gratified by his appointment as governor of the Netherlands. Though not a military genius, he had energy and ability, and on his way to the Netherlands at the head of an army, he had a chance to prove his mettle at his very first trial.

At that time the fortunes of the branch of the Habsburgs in South Germany were at a low ebb because Cardinal Richelieu had subsidized the King of Sweden to intervene against them. The Habsburg forces had been heavily defeated, first by Sweden's warrior King Gustavus Adolphus and then, after his death in battle, by the army he had created. Cardinal Infant Ferdinand marched his army to South Germany, linked up with the troops of his Habsburg cousin, Ferdinand, King of Hungary, and confronted the Swedish army and its German Protestant allies at Nördlingen, near the Danube, in September 1634. The Habsburg forces won a total victory. Much of the Swedish army surrendered; the German allies fled, and Habsburg authority was re-established in South Germany. Entering the Spanish Netherlands after this impressive victory, the Cardinal Infant was greeted as a savior, a new champion who might yet defeat the rebellious Dutch and restore to the South its past greatness and prosperity.

Antwerp's city fathers turned, of course, to Rubens to design the triumphal arches for the city's official reception. As a young man working with Otto van Veen, Rubens had helped to design the pageant of welcome for the Archduchess and her husband; now he was asked to make Ferdinand's reception a still more glorious occasion. But time was short: "I am so overburdened with the preparations for the triumphal entry of the Cardinal Infant," Rubens wrote to Peiresc in December 1634, "that I have time neither to live nor to write. . . . The magistrates of this city have laid upon my shoulders the entire burden of this festival, and I believe you would not be displeased at the invention and variety of subjects, the novelty of the designs and the fitness of their application."

It was the custom to use occasions of this kind for propagating political ideas. Rubens' designs had a threefold purpose: to glorify the House of Habsburg as the legitimate ruler of the Netherlands, to advertise the qualities of the new governor and to draw his attention to the declining condition of Antwerp. As he traversed the city the Cardinal Infant would go through a semicircular portico adorned with the figures of all his distinguished ancestors, and pass under several others that celebrated his recent victory at Nördlingen. Last of all he would be confronted by an allegory of Antwerp: Mercury, patron of merchants and traders, was to be seen poised for departure while sad groups of allegorical figures mourned the decline of their city, bereft of commerce and prosperity by the long war and the Dutch blockade.

Time was short for the preparation of this ambitious scheme; Rubens, working at top speed, completed the designs for the arches, colonnades and all the figures in 15 days. After that the architectural structures were fashioned out of wood and canvas, while the scenes and figures were painted with the help of friends and pupils. Among them were the vigorous Jacob Jordaens, by now one of Antwerp's most successful painters, and a young man named Erasmus Quellin, who was generally considered the most talented assistant in the Rubens studio.

But as always when there was need for haste, the master did much of the work himself. His picture of the meeting between the Cardinal Infant and his imperial cousin on the eve of the battle of Nördlingen is a masterpiece of dramatic historical painting. It was typical of Rubens that even in a picture boldly designed to be effective at a distance he gave careful attention to the individual character of the officers attendant on the two princes.

Yet despite the vigor with which he tackled the project, Rubens felt the onset of age. He had been occasionally troubled by gout in the past and now his old enemy returned with increasing frequency. When the Cardinal Infant made his formal entry to Antwerp, Rubens was too ill to attend the ceremonies. The tactful prince visited him in his home to thank him for his work; though he had no personal pretension to being a connoisseur, he had been instructed by his brother the King to lose no opportunity of acquiring anything from the hand of Rubens.

A few months before Rubens began the designs for the reception of the Cardinal Infant, the nine canvases for the King of England's Banqueting House had been finished and placed on view in his studio. But Charles had neither paid nor sent for them. Balthasar Gerbier, who had now been appointed the King's official representative in Brussels, reported to the King that this delay was causing malicious gossip to the effect that the King could not afford what he had commissioned. In spite of the broad hint, Charles delayed another 14 months before he finally sent for the pictures. He was delighted with them when they arrived but still had difficulty in finding the money. The £3,000 payment came at last, two and a half years later, and was followed a year after that by a present of a gold chain.

The ceiling of the Banqueting House *(page 140)* stands comparison with the greatest works of Tintoretto and Veronese in Venice. During the previous century the Venetians had brought to perfection the sumptuous treatment of ceilings, both in churches and in palaces. They did not cover them with frescoes but designed instead a richly carved and gilded wooden framework into which painted canvases were inserted. Such a ceiling had been designed by Whitehall's architect, Inigo Jones, who had studied in Venice just as intensely as Rubens had done.

King James I, whose reign was the subject of Rubens' paintings, had been the first king to inherit the Crowns of both England and Scotland, and so to unite Great Britain. This may well have had a special appeal for Rubens, who had striven so long and vainly to re-unite his own divided Netherlands. At any rate he illustrated the union of the Crowns in a composition of lyrical beauty. The King leans benevolently toward his infant son and successor, Charles, who is supported by two buxom nymphs, representing England and Scotland.

This subject fills one of the three large canvases in the central section of the ceiling. It is balanced by an allegorical representation of the King conferring the benefits of Peace and Justice, while in the central panel James is borne to heaven among a bevy of angels and virtues. In the four corners of the ceiling smaller pictures represent the triumph of Wisdom, Reason and Liberality over Disorder and Vice, while the sides of the ceiling are adorned with two long panels of flying, tumbling cherubs.

This grandiose work, remarkable for its dynamic force and rich harmony of color, is still intact and in its original position. It has recently been revealed in something like its initial splendor by a careful restoration not only of the pictures but of the vast room of which it is the crowning glory. The color is as Venetian as the conception—warm reds are balanced by luminous yellows and vibrant greens, lightened by the cool, pale tints of sky and flowers and the rosy radiance of the nymphs and cherubs. The nine pictures are so co-ordinated that at first glance they strike the beholder as a single, majestic work of art.

When Charles finally sent for the pictures in July 1635, Rubens was 58 years old—too old, he felt, to involve himself ever again in the busy atmosphere of a court. "Inasmuch as I have a horror of courts, I sent my work to England in the hands of someone else," he wrote to Peiresc. He might have enjoyed seeing his pictures elevated to their proper setting, but not at the price of the wearisome formalities involved in attendance at Whitehall.

He had much to content him in his domestic life. Hélène's third child, a daughter, was born in this year and baptized Isabella Hélène. At about the same time Rubens painted the portrait of his former father-in-law, Jan Brant. His second marriage had not disturbed his relations with his first wife's family, and the naming of his little daughter after both his wives was indicative of this.

But more and more Rubens felt the need to withdraw from Antwerp's crowded swirl and professional activity, and to lead a quieter, less exacting life with more time to paint for his private pleasure. Like most prosperous townsmen of his day, he had always had small investments in land out in the country—a farm or two or a little manor house—and he had sometimes visited these for relaxation. But now he decided to have a country residence where he could live at ease for a good part of the year. He settled on the Château de Steen *(page 185)*, a country manor house in the Flemish Renaissance style of the mid-16th Century. It was described some years later as comprising a "large house and other fine buildings in the form of a castle, with gardens, orchard, fruit trees and drawbridge, and a large hillock on the middle of which stands a high square tower, having also a lake and a farm with farmhouse, barns, diverse stables and outbuildings, the whole surrounded by a moat."

He planned in the future to spend several months of every year at this country house with Hélène. It was near enough to Antwerp and Brussels for their friends to visit them. They would not be lonely. The studio could be left for a few months at a time to the care of his assistants. At the Château de Steen he could find the liberty and quietness of spirit that he needed and that he felt he had earned. Here he could enjoy the simple pleasures of the countryside, watch the wheat fields ripening, the cattle grazing, the country folk at work and play.

Rubens had been interested in landscape art since his youth in Italy and he had sometimes painted country scenes, carefully finished pieces or rapid sketches, as mood and opportunity varied; on his last visit to Spain he had done a swift and striking impression of a windstorm. He had been fascinated by Elsheimer's landscapes in his youth and by Adriaen Brouwer's work in more recent years. He also deeply admired the work of "Old" Bruegel (as Pieter Bruegel was called), the father of Rubens' friend Jan Brueghel, and the greatest interpreter of Flemish peasant life; Rubens possessed no fewer than 12 of his pictures. But, though Rubens' own occasional sketches had revealed an observation of peasant life, the pressure of his commissions for allegorical and decorative works, for altarpieces, tapestry designs and portraits, had left him with very little time to develop this interest.

Thus it was no desire for inactive retirement that caused Rubens to buy the Château de Steen. On the contrary, he looked forward to a new and calmer period of work, in surroundings that would enable him to develop talents he had hitherto neglected.

The Robust
Form

Rubens' joyous spirit emerges nowhere so clearly as in his portrayals of the nude female. Erotic, as all nudes should be, sensual but not lascivious, wholesome but never banal, his nudes bear the mark of his own hearty pleasure in life. It is no contradiction that Rubens, the greatest religious painter of his time, was also its greatest master of the female form. In his view, the human body was every bit as much a work of God as the life of the holiest saint, and although he often placed his nudes amid settings of the pagan past, he painted them with a forthrightness that reflects his strong religious conviction.

Technically, it is almost impossible to find fault with a nude by Rubens, although modern tastes in feminine beauty are considerably different from his. He preferred plump models not only because they were closer to the ideals of his time, but because a well-fleshed body with its subtle surface hollows, swells and curves was more interesting to paint. Rubens probably understood better than any painter in history how to achieve the extraordinarily delicate nuances of red, blue, white and yellow that make up the color of flesh; Rubens' women, it has been said, seem to be composed of milk and blood. In addition to being a brilliant colorist, Rubens was a master at depicting subtleties of texture, and the structure of the body. With his predecessor Titian and his successor Renoir, he is unsurpassed as a painter of the human form.

This early nude reflects Rubens' studies of Italian art. The subject was borrowed from Titian, and the figure, statuesque and solid, is reminiscent of Michelangelo's giantesses. But the vitality of the body, the modeling of flesh and the vibrant color are Rubens' own.

The Toilet of Venus, 1612-1615

152

153

Like all his works, Rubens' nudes are filled with energy, communicating his own love of life. This painting, showing an orgiastic ritual centering on a marble statue of Venus, is a glorious summary of his skills: men, women and children, architecture, landscape, animals, drapery are bathed in soft light. The scene also pays brilliant homage to Titian, whose bacchanals Rubens studied so carefully that they became part of his own visual vocabulary.

In Rubens' painting, three main groups balance the composition. At the center, before a statue that seems almost alive, a maiden offers a sacrifice in a glowing brazier, while another proffers a mirror and a third adjusts the statue's diaphanous drapery. Above, cherubs garland the trees with ripe fruit beneath a rich red canopy; in the foreground and at the right others dance around the pedestal, while two women bring statuettes in homage to love and a satyr leads two dancers into the woods.

The most important group is at left. Here is love incarnate; three muscular satyrs cavort with maidens lost in the delirium of Venus' spell. And here is a clue to Rubens' inspiration; the girl at the far left is unmistakably the artist's young second wife, Hélène. Rubens' celebration of her beauty *(detail, overleaf)*, and his love shine throughout this work.

The Feast of Venus, c. 1630-1640

154

Rape of the Daughters of Leucippus, c. 1619

Two major paintings reveal the changing aspects of Rubens' portrayal of the nude between the vigorous middle of his career and his later life. The work above, in which the mythological half-brothers Castor and Pollux abduct the daughters of a king of Messene, swirls with Baroque excitement. The contrasting surfaces of polished armor, horsehair, silk and flesh, enliven the picture with textures that are almost palpable. The generous curves of the pinwheel composition are echoed within the figures themselves, whose every dimple seems delineated.

By contrast, the placid dance of Venus' handmaidens *(right)* suggests the older artist's mellowed, more reflective turn of mind. Painted within a year of his death, the picture presents Rubens' ideal of feminine beauty. The composition, a variant of a pose established by Greco-Roman sculptors and painted by such Renaissance masters as Botticelli and Raphael, is invested with all the energy and force that Rubens usually spent on elaborate compositions. But now he has enclosed the force of life itself within the forms of the three nudes.

The Three Graces, 1639

Details from these two works are reproduced on the next four
pages. Overleaf is the central portion of *Rape of the Daughters
of Leucippus*; following that is a section from *The Three Graces*.

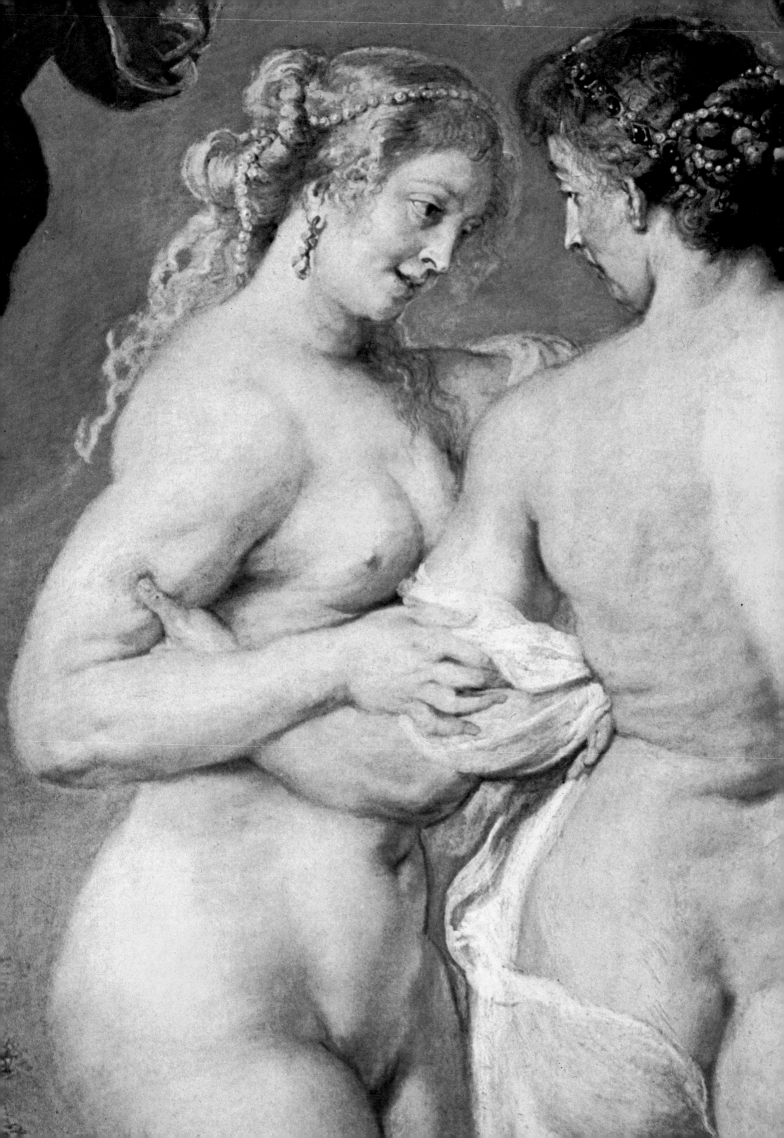

VIII

A Lasting
Vigor

The chief joy of Rubens' later years was his wife, Hélène Fourment, a beautiful girl from a good Antwerp family. Rubens celebrated her charms in this warm, uninhibited work, which he painted for himself and willed to Hélène so it would not leave the family. As he had done many times before, Rubens borrowed from Titian the idea of juxtaposing the pale opalescence of flesh with the darker tones of fur and fabric.

The Little Fur, c. 1638

Soon after he bought the Château de Steen, 18 miles south of Antwerp, Rubens began seriously applying his art to the surrounding country and its people. Even before he moved he had, in about 1630, produced a major work that reflected this interest. It is a scene of a joyous peasant feast, generally known as *La Kermesse (pages 180-181)*. This traditional Netherlands festival was a theme that the great Pieter Bruegel, whom Rubens admired so much, had often and realistically painted in the previous century.

Rubens did not idealize Flemish peasants any more than Bruegel had done. His revelers are sturdy creatures whose movements he has accurately observed, and whose behavior is a logical part of the country scene. He chose to show his admiration for their lusty cheerfulness and for their zest for life rather than dwell on the squalor of their existence or the sufferings imposed on them by plague, famine and war. The exuberant *La Kermesse* can be regarded as Rubens' tribute to the unquenchable vitality of his humbler compatriots.

But as he came to love the countryside around his château, Rubens concentrated more and more in his painting on the landscape itself. One of his most beautiful treatments of this subject is a view of his mansion, the *Château de Steen (pages 182-183)*. The flat green country, broken by tree-fringed streams and sparse woodlands, stretches away to lose itself in a blue horizon. The evening light strikes aslant through a group of tall trees onto the mellow façade and the glinting windowpanes of the great house at the extreme left of the picture. The birds, the wild flowers, the branches and the foliage are painted with remarkable precision, but the detail of the foreground is perfectly subordinated to the rest of the picture. It is a faithful representation of the Flemish countryside. No doubt Rubens selected and composed some of the details, but nothing is romanticized; if it were not for the magic of the light the painting would be a prosaic, almost a documentary, statement. But sunlight glorifies every landscape, even the most commonplace. Rubens, with his passion for the transforming beauty of light, had found in landscape painting another sphere to explore. The soft radiance of summer evenings enthralled and challenged him; again and again he captured or set out to capture the transient glow, sometimes even venturing to paint the sun itself effulgent between banks of cloud.

Other effects of light also interested him, such as the sudden clarity of the air after rain. In his *Landscape with a Rainbow,* the foreground, with cattle, haymakers and girls returning from the field, is bright, while mist and rain veil the bluish distances of the fertile lowlands.

He painted landscapes for his own pleasure and interest, making explorations in technique, seeking to show nature unadorned—not modified to suit the fashion, heightened to theatrical effects or toned down to the light of a studio. "In no other branch of the art is Rubens greater than in landscape," wrote the English landscape painter John Constable, who went on to praise "the freshness and dewy light, the joyous and animated character" that Rubens imparted to "the level, monotonous scenery of Flanders." Constable's famous picture *The Hay Wain* was strongly influenced by Rubens. Exhibited in the Paris Salon of 1824, it became a turning point in 19th Century landscape painting. Thus the influence of the landscape studies that Rubens did in his last years stretched far into the future.

Rubens' contentment during these years was enhanced by the turn of national affairs. For the time being, at least, the fortunes of the Spanish Netherlands had improved under the energetic leadership of the young governor, Cardinal Infant Ferdinand, who seemed at first to be as successful a general as Spinola had been. The King of France had recently declared war on Spain, which meant that the luckless Spanish Netherlands was open to attack not only from the Dutch but also on its French frontier. The French and Dutch armies actually combined in their attack; but Ferdinand repelled the invasion, winning a series of important victories. The most notable was his victory at Calloo in 1638, in honor of which Antwerp staged a triumphal procession; Rubens, once again asked to contribute to the decorations, and as pleased by the victory as any of his countrymen, designed a gloriously emblazoned chariot.

But Rubens would much have preferred a truce to hostilities. "I am a peace-loving man," he wrote Peiresc, "I believe that it ought to be the first wish of every honest man to live in tranquillity of mind. . . . I am sorry that all kings and princes are not of this humor." Since that could not be true, however, it was obviously more comfortable to be on the winning side. As Rubens, not without patriotic pride, informed Peiresc in the same letter, "Here public affairs have changed their aspect; from a defensive war we have passed with great advantage to the offensive." Thanks to the skill of the Cardinal Infant, Rubens was able, during his last years, to continue enjoying this comforting illusion. Only after his death did his country, ruinously entangled in the falling fortunes of Spain, plunge to irrevocable defeat.

Hopeful about public affairs, and enjoying his well-earned leisure, Rubens had time for other interests besides landscape painting and the observation of peasant life. In spite of the state of war between their two countries he was still in friendly correspondence with Peiresc about not only Classical antiquities but also the optical effect of color and other scientific subjects. Apart from his special interest in optics, Rubens' scientific tastes were the fashionable ones of his time, including a continuing curiosity about the possibilities of a "perpetual motion" machine.

But, as always, his keenest attention was devoted to Classical and early Christian antiquity. Rubens was therefore overjoyed when Peiresc sent him a copy of a rare figure composition that had survived from Classical times. It was the *Aldobrandini Wedding,* a Roman wall painting that had been discovered during excavations while Rubens was in Rome 30 years before. "You could not have made me a present more acceptable, or one that conformed more to my taste and my desire," he wrote to Peiresc. He, in turn, had exciting news to pass on to his friend. On his own property, at the Château de Steen, his peasants were constantly turning up "ancient medals, mostly of the Antonines, in bronze and silver." He was naturally delighted with these souvenirs of the Roman Empire under the Second Century Emperors Antoninus Pius and his successors. Rubens was particularly pleased that the first two medals that came into his possession bore the inscriptions *Spes* and *Victoria:* Hope and Victory. He could not but think it a good omen.

During these last leisurely years, Rubens embarked on one final book of engravings, a superb collection of heads of Roman emperors and philosophers, which he drew with detailed care from busts or casts that he owned himself or borrowed from friends. Apart from this venture, he did no more illustrations for Balthasar Moretus at the Plantin press, feeling that he must conserve his energies for more important work. But he did not wholly abandon his collaboration with his lifelong friend; he handed over the task to Erasmus Quellin, at this time his senior assistant, and supplied him with ideas.

This did not mean that Rubens abandoned his professional career. He was still in his studio at Antwerp for at least half the year, working on commissions as before. Some of his most eloquent artistic comments on man's inhumanity to man date from this closing decade of his life. They are all the more powerful because of the limpid daylight with which he now suffused every subject. His earlier religious paintings had been strongly influenced by Tintoretto and Caravaggio, whose heavy shadows and fierce contrasts of light and darkness seemed particularly suited to tragic themes. But now for Rubens light more and more became the essential factor. Color, projection, depth—all these he interpreted by the subtlest interplay of light. Now his canvases had no dark shadows, no large masses of color, but instead were filled with exquisitely varied and delicate gradations of tints and tones. It was in this manner, sunlit and luminous, that he now depicted the Passion of Christ or the sufferings of the saints.

Such was the picture, the *Martyrdom of St. Livinus,* that he painted for the high altar of the Jesuit church in Ghent. The saint, a missionary bishop of the Seventh Century, had been murdered, according to legend, by the heathen inhabitants of the Netherlands. Rubens showed him as a venerable figure in episcopal robes. The barbarians have forced him to his knees; one of them grasps him by the beard, another by the belt, a third, a savage brute in a red cap, has torn out his tongue. The saint,

After Cardinal Infant Ferdinand won a victory for the Spanish Netherlands over the Dutch at Calloo in 1638, Antwerp staged a triumphal welcome for him; Rubens designed the decorations, as he had when Ferdinand first came to the country *(page 148).* His oil sketch for a parade chariot shows figures representing the city, Victory, Triumph, Virtue and Fortune, and two bound captives. The chariot—a top view of which is seen in the upper left-hand corner of the sketch—was such a success that it was used in Antwerp's annual processions for several decades after Rubens' death.

167

his robes spattered with blood, looks up ashen-faced to heaven, where a flight of avenging angels appears in the clouds. A soldier in the foreground starts back in amazement at the vision, while others stare at the opening skies and a white horse rears up in terror. The central incident of martyrdom is treated with relentless realism. It could be the torturing of any helpless captive by the brutal mercenaries of the Thirty Years' War. Take away the miraculous vision in the heavens and the picture is as unflinching in its realism as the work of Jacques Callot, whose etchings, *Miseries and Misfortunes of War,* are the best known contemporary indictment of the horrors of 17th Century warfare.

Another picture on a tragic theme painted during these years is the *Massacre of the Innocents.* Pieter Brueghel in the previous century had treated the subject as though it were a current event. In Brueghel's famous picture, troops with pikes and halberds storm through a Flemish village hunting the children and their screaming mothers out of the thatched cottages. Rubens, more historically minded, set the scene on the steps of a classical palace such as might have existed in Romanized Judea. But the feeling that he brought to the subject was as contemporary as Brueghel's. On either side of the picture is a struggling group of women and soldiers, the mothers biting and clawing at the murderers in frenzied defense of the children. In the center a dreadful quiet reigns, for here the struggle is over. A standing woman, lost to everything but her grief, embraces her dead child. Another, monumental in silent anguish, lifts her child's bloodstained shirt to heaven in mute appeal. The sunshine that illuminates the dreadful scene, the light colors of draperies and sky enhance the horror—as if to remind us that such things happen not only under cover of darkness but also under the hand of authority and in God's clear daylight.

In painting subjects like these Rubens did not have to rely on imagination. The sufferings of war were never far away from his home. As a boy he had seen the burned and ruined buildings of Antwerp, gaunt reminders of the rioting of Spanish troops within the city walls in 1576. There was war in his own country during the greater part of his life; hungry refugees from the stricken areas and maimed soldiers begging in the streets would have been familiar spectacles to him. Across the eastern border in the Rhineland, tragic conditions prevailed because of the recurrent fighting of the Thirty Years' War. In 1636 an attendant of the Earl of Arundel described towns, villages and castles as being all "battered, pillaged and burnt," and told of the charity dispensed to the starving at Rüdesheim and to poor wretches lying on dunghills at Mainz, scarcely able to crawl to receive it.

Yet when Rubens set out to comment on a modern political theme, he followed the usual fashion of his day and adopted the allegorical method. About two years after finishing the *Massacre of the Innocents,* he painted his now famous picture, *The Horrors of War,* for the Grand Duke of Tuscany. In a letter to the Duke's court painter, Justus Sustermans, he elucidated its message: "The principal figure is Mars who . . . rushes forth with shield and bloodstained sword, threatening the people with great disaster. He pays little heed to Venus, his mistress, who

. . . strives with caresses and embraces to hold him. . . . Nearby are monsters personifying Pestilence and Famine, those inseparable partners of War. . . . You will find under the feet of Mars a book as well as a drawing on paper, to imply that he treads underfoot all the arts and letters. . . . The grief-stricken woman clothed in black, with torn veil, robbed of all her jewels and other ornaments, is the unfortunate Europe who, for so many years now, has suffered plunder, outrage and misery."

It is a dynamic and ingenious composition, though as a comment on suffering and disaster it has, at least to the modern mind, much less force than the *Massacre of the Innocents*. But in the background there is a group with a mother and child that is authentic and timeless. These could be any refugees in any bombardment, and the 20th Century has seen the mother's face and gesture a hundred times in newsreels.

In 1636 King Philip IV of Spain commissioned Rubens to undertake a work of quite another sort: an immense scheme of decoration for the Torre de la Parada, a new summer palace and hunting lodge near Madrid. The King wanted a comprehensive series of pictures illustrating all the fantastic and fabulous legends of antiquity enshrined in the *Metamorphoses* of Ovid. Apart from a few decorative panels of hunting dogs and game, the designs were all to be by Rubens.

It was an exciting and absorbing task. Rubens had often painted such scenes individually before, and no living artist knew more about the legends of the ancient world or had studied their representation in statues, sarcophagi, coins and gems with greater attention. Now, finally, he had the glorious prospect of creating his own interpretation of the whole abundant world inhabited by gods and goddesses, heroes and titans, nymphs and satyrs.

Inevitably his thoughts went back to the Duke of Mantua's Palazzo del Te, where in his youth he had admired, studied and sketched the decorative masterpieces of Giulio Romano. There, too, the legends of antiquity had been painted on walls and ceilings; from time to time in Rubens' work for the King of Spain a remembered figure or group appears transmuted. Giulio had painted a magical figure of Venus standing at the edge of the sea wringing the water out of her long hair. When Rubens sketched the birth of Venus for the King of Spain's palace he copied this gesture. But his Venus, instead of standing motionless at the sea's edge, runs lightly out of the shallow waves. It is as though Giulio's goddess had been startled into graceful movement by the sound of the conch shell blown by the sea god whom Rubens depicted rising from the surf close behind her.

It was with this commission that the aging Rubens took advantage of his enormous prestige in Antwerp's artistic community by calling on some of the city's leading painters to help carry out the full-sized pictures from his sketches *(pages 178-179)*. Such was the efficiency of this method that 56 canvases were packed up and dispatched to Madrid within 15 months. A second large consignment went off a year later, and still the King ordered more.

Although Rubens' health was now beginning to fail, he worked on assiduously, and the freshness of his imagination showed no signs of flagging. But the arthritic pains, at that time vaguely called gout, that had plagued him on and off for many years became more frequent and by an evil chance settled in his right hand. At times he was unable to take up a pencil or a brush, a deprivation more tormenting than any physical pain. In the autumn of 1638 he fell seriously ill; by December his life was despaired of and he received extreme unction. But he made an astonishing recovery and was hard at work again in the new year.

Cardinal Infant Ferdinand came several times to see how the work for the Torre de la Parada was progressing and, although he knew very little about painting, he did his best to describe the pictures in letters to the King, his brother. He was impressed by the frank and joyful beauty of a large *Judgment of Paris,* though he was not quite sure that he approved of the life-sized naked goddesses. Would they not be better with a little more drapery? Rubens gave him to understand that it was too late to make any alterations, and the picture went off to Spain in spite of Ferdinand's misgivings—which were not shared by the King.

Rubens still displayed a versatile command of his art. It was probably in his last year that he painted one more self-portrait *(page 184).* The picture is direct and uncompromising; he shows himself as an old man, looking older, in fact, than his 60-odd years. His beard and mustache are noticeably thin, and the carefully curled hair showing under the broad-brimmed hat could be a wig. His expression is withdrawn, a little world-weary, but the eyes, though they have lost their eagerness, are clear and keen. Nothing, one feels, would escape that penetrating glance. His left hand, powerful and well-shaped, rests on the hilt of an elegant sword, perhaps the gift presented him by Charles I. The right hand is concealed in a thick glove: with swollen arthritic joints it was no longer beautiful. Nor was it always the dexterous and unfailing servant of his craft. Yet not in this portrait nor in any other of Rubens' last pictures did the crippling of his right hand affect his mastery; there were days when he did not paint at all, but there were never days when he painted badly.

Possibly because he feared his hand might soon fail him altogether, he took up a new kind of designing in his last years. A young sculptor named Lucas Fayd'herbe had joined his studio in 1637, because of, as Rubens put it, "the relationship that exists between our arts of painting and sculpture." Fayd'herbe had a delicate talent and Rubens began to employ him to execute small works in ivory from his designs. In collaboration they produced an ivory crucifix, a group of ivory children and an ivory Cupid and Psyche asleep on a couch.

The story of Cupid and Psyche came into Rubens' mind in another context when his old friend Gerbier, still representing Charles I of England at Brussels, asked him on behalf of the King to decorate the pretty little palace he had just built at Greenwich, near London, for his Queen. Jordaens had submitted designs that were not altogether satisfactory and the King clearly preferred the prospect of securing more work from Rubens. But his Cupid and Psyche for the Queen of England was never to be painted. Subject and price were settled only a few days before his death.

In March 1640 the arthritic trouble in his hand returned. Though much hindered in his painting, he could still dictate letters. On April 17 he

Even before his partial retirement to the country in 1630, Rubens showed a keen interest in rural scenes. This sketch of a milkmaid and cow was made about 1620 and may well have been the basis for several such groups that appear in his landscape paintings of later years; it was Rubens' habit to make sketches from life in black chalk, to go over them in ink and then to save them for use in a painting.

wrote to an old friend in Rome, the Flemish sculptor François Duquesnoy, who had just completed the colossal statue of St. Andrew that stands to this day under the dome of St. Peter's: "I hear the praises for the statue of St. Andrew, just unveiled, and I along with all our nation rejoice and participate in your fame. If I were not detained by age, and by gout which renders me useless, I should go there to enjoy with my own eyes and admire the perfection of works so worthy."

Rubens would never see Rome again; but he did have plans to leave Antwerp for the Château de Steen when spring came. Meanwhile he congratulated his young friend Lucas Fayd'herbe on his marriage: "My wife and I, with both my sons, sincerely wish you and your beloved every happiness and complete, long-lasting contentment in marriage. There is no hurry about the little ivory child; you now have other child-work of greater importance on hand. But your visit will always be very welcome to us."

This is Rubens' last known letter, written on May 9, 1640, a genial, affectionate letter rejoicing in the happiness of the younger generation. It is pleasant to imagine that as he wrote it his mind may have reverted to that marriage picture he had painted, 30 years before, of Isabella and himself in a honeysuckle bower. He had been singularly fortunate; he had known "complete, long-lasting contentment" twice over in marriage. He wrote his last letter with all his family gathered in his home, his wife, their children and his two grown-up sons. Summer was coming and with it perhaps relief from the crippling pain in his right hand. Soon he would visit his beloved Château de Steen, where the fertile country would offer him an ever-changing harmony of light and color. He had exciting work on his hands—*Perseus and Andromeda* for the King of Spain nearly finished, a commission for a church in Cologne, the projected Cupid and Psyche for the Queen of England. . . .

But on the last day of May 1640 Balthasar Gerbier wrote from Brussels to a friend in England, "Sir Peter Rubens is deadly sick, the physicians of this town being sent unto him for to try their best skill on him." The doctors from Brussels arrived too late. On that same day in the evening Gerbier wrote again, this time directly to the King of England: "News is come of Sir Peter Rubens' death."

Rubens had died in his house in Antwerp on May 30, 1640, the crippling disease having finally caused his heart to fail. He was not quite 63 years old. He was fortunate in his death as he had been in his life. He did not outlive his skill or his creative power or his fame. Nor did he live to see the fatal end of the war that ruined his country.

He was buried with due solemnity in his parish church of St. Jacques in Antwerp, and his friends and colleagues were entertained, in the fashion of the day, at three large funeral banquets. More than 500 Masses were sung in the churches and convents of the Netherlands, which he had filled with his great pictures. Some years later Hélène Fourment carried out his wishes by building a memorial chapel at St. Jacques for him and his descendants. A graceful Madonna in marble by Lucas Fayd'herbe stands over the altar; and under the statue hangs the picture that, on his deathbed, Rubens had assigned to that place.

The painting still hangs there *(pages 68-69)*, the *Madonna with Saints*, done a short time before he died. It is an unconventional, pleasing, puzzling picture, lovely in color but overcrowded with figures and symbols, as though he had not fully worked out all that he wanted to convey about the material and spiritual duties of man, and about the faith that had been, all his life, so important a source of inspiration. The exact significance of his choice of figures is not clear—St. George with sword and banner, St. Jerome with book and lion, the Magdalen and three others who cannot be identified. But the Virgin and Child are among the loveliest he ever painted. The Child offers a small hand to a venerable worshiper while turning his head back to look at his mother. It is one of the most endearing of his many studies of small children and was perhaps drawn from his youngest son, Peter Paul, who was only three years old at his father's death.

Rubens left his family rich, and it became richer still a few months later from the proceeds of the sale of his antiquities and of the paintings remaining in his studio. Hélène, then only 26, was not long in marrying again. The rest of her life, the longer part of it, seems to have been uneventful and, given her temperament and her comfortable situation, presumably happy. Albert, Nicolas and the five children of his second marriage pursued their unspectacular lives as respected citizens; Albert and perhaps Nicolas as well held civic office in Antwerp.

Rubens had always hoped one of his children might inherit part of his talent. Albert and Nicolas were 25 and 22 when their father died, and had no interest in painting. But his and Hélène's eldest child, Clara Johanna, was still only eight, and another daughter, Constantia-Albertina, was born to Hélène eight months after her husband died. There was also their other daughter, Isabella Hélène, age five, and the two little boys, Frans, six, and Peter Paul, three. In his will, therefore, Rubens directed that his immense collection of studies and drawings—an invaluable treasury of ideas for any practicing painter—be kept intact in case any of his sons should follow in his footsteps or any of his daughters marry a painter. They were to be sold only when it was clear beyond doubt that they would be of no practical use to any of his children. This became evident finally when Constantia-Albertina entered a convent at age 16, and in 1657 the last of his drawings were sold at auction.

"Jordaens is now the prime painter of Antwerp," wrote Balthasar Gerbier, a few days after the death of Rubens. He proved right in this statement, although the pre-eminence of Jordaens did not at first go unchallenged. Erasmus Quellin, left in charge of Rubens' studio, strove hard but vainly to equal his master in completing the pictures for the King of Spain. He was, actually, a decorative painter of considerable merit, and was appointed to succeed Rubens as the chief designer for all civic functions and processions in Antwerp; but he could not follow Rubens in the multitudinous other spheres of his activity.

For a brief space Anthony van Dyck competed. He had been thought of as the heir apparent in his youth, but much had happened since then. He had been away from Antwerp for the best part of seven years, had taken a noble wife and appeared to have settled for good at the court of

Charles I. He had developed a graceful, aristocratic style in portraiture that was to set the tone in England for many years and exert great influence over Reynolds and Gainsborough in the ensuing century. He had become a colorist of the most delicate subtlety and had begun to evolve an original and mysteriously poetic style in the small decorative paintings that he sometimes did for King Charles.

By 1640, however, political unrest in England threatened the court on which van Dyck depended, and he was beset by anxieties about his future. He returned to Antwerp a few months after the death of Rubens. The Cardinal Infant suggested that he take over the management of the still unfinished series of pictures for the King of Spain. But van Dyck had been working for too many years in his own independent manner and found it difficult to take over another man's ideas—even those of Rubens. Furthermore, after his long residence in a country where he was the only artist of any real importance, it was not easy for him to fit in once again with the numerous painters of Antwerp.

So he moved on to Paris, where massive redecoration of the Louvre was in progress. But Louis XIII had recently succeeded in tempting Nicolas Poussin back from Rome and was not interested in employing van Dyck too. Ill and disillusioned, he returned to London, where political turmoil had caused the arts to be forgotten. Van Dyck had long before chosen as his personal emblem the sunflower, that bold, brilliant disc of gold that always turns toward the sun. Prematurely, the sun had set for him. His health and spirits broken, he died in his 43rd year, in December 1641, just 18 months after Rubens. So it was indeed the boisterous, opulent Jordaens who for the next 30 years dominated the Antwerp School.

Seventeen quick sketches of a dancing peasant couple cover a sheet of studies made from life by Rubens about 1636. With spare strokes of chalk, which he later accentuated with ink, Rubens captured the energetic contortions of the swiftly moving bodies. The perspective of these figures, some of which appear in Rubens' painting *La Kermesse (pages 180-181),* suggests that the artist may have observed the scene from the upper floor of an inn.

The history of art has no instance to show of so universal an influence, so absolute an authority and so complete a triumph." With these words the 19th Century biographer of Rubens, Max Rooses, summed up the painter's lifework.

It was an extraordinary career, not the least because there is never at any point in the work of Rubens a sense of finality. He was still experimenting and exploring at the time of his death. He had begun as a Flemish Romanist under Otto van Veen; he had drunk deeply of many influences in Italy, ancient and modern, and had brought back to the Netherlands an imaginative interpretation of the new style, the Baroque, which he helped create. Strongly influenced by Raphael, by the Venetians, by the turbulent invention of Giulio Romano and by the decorous classical manner of Carracci as well as the dramatic realism of Caravaggio, Rubens' composition was skillfully balanced, massive and powerful, his colors were rich and velvety. But his great *Descent from the Cross* in Antwerp's cathedral, finished when he was 37, had revealed a growing subtlety in the use of color, and a heightened sensibility to light, which gradually became the principal element in his work.

Rubens enjoyed his fame, but was not corrupted by it. He could learn late in life not only from direct observation of nature, but from the work of other men younger than himself. While fulfilling a mass of commissions that would have exhausted a lesser man, he still had time to study landscape painting for his own delight, and to learn to capture with his brush the unending interplay of light, color and form in the fields and woods of Flanders.

An achievement so broad, an artistic vision of such individuality and power could not fail to exercise an influence for many generations. Equally, it could not fail to provoke opposition. In the three centuries since Rubens' death he has been extravagantly praised and resentfully criticized. He has never been ignored.

The attack began in France, a generation after his death, with the disparagement by some critics of his tempestuous vision and kaleidoscope of colors; they preferred the firm outline and geometrical style that they associated with Nicolas Poussin. Other French critics rushed to Rubens' defense. A quarrel between the "Rubenists" and the "Poussinists" was launched—and it has still not been resolved. Reduced to its essentials, the argument concerns the rival claims of color and line. The Poussinists set the highest value on line, on drawing, as having an absolute value in the art of representing things. Color, they argued, was of no importance because it depended on light and was therefore accidental, variable and, so to speak, not "true." The accidental and variable quality of color was, of course, its attraction for Rubens, as it has been for many later painters. The Rubenists wanted to paint what they saw; the Poussinists pursued a perfected ideal of form. The quarrel is as much a disagreement of temperament as of vision, and we can trace it up to modern times. Thus the Impressionists can be seen as Rubenists, and certain of our more austere abstract painters as Poussinists.

Over the years, Rubens' reputation has been affected by many variations of the central theme of this argument. He has been admired in epochs when Romanticism has been dominant, disparaged when formal Classicism has been the fashion. Immensely admired for the greater part of the 19th Century, his work declined in popularity after the First World War. As the intellectual climate grew more chilly and the confident belief in progress gave way to the doubts and anxieties of our present complex and threatened societies, Rubens' emphasis on material beauty and his immense assurance had less appeal. His spiritual insight was also less apparent to those who could not share his serene faith.

On the other hand, Rubens' work has had an enormous effect on painters of many different kinds through the years. Antoine Watteau, born 44 years after Rubens died, passionately loved Rubens' work, and at the end of his own life wrote with extravagant pleasure of a small Rubens original that had been brought to him: "From the moment I received it, I have not had a moment's repose, and my eyes can never weary of returning toward the easel where I have placed it as if in a shrine."

In the late 18th Century Sir Joshua Reynolds filled his notebook with comments on Rubens while touring the churches and galleries of the Netherlands. He regretted that Rubens lacked the elegance and the refinement that the 18th Century valued, but he was lost in admiration of his technique: "He possessed the true art of imitating. He saw the objects of nature with a painter's eye; he saw at once the predominant feature by which every object is known and distinguished: and as soon as seen, it was executed with a facility that is astonishing. . . . Rubens was, perhaps, the greatest master in the mechanical part of the art, and the best work-man with his tools that ever exercised a pencil. This power, which Rubens possessed in the highest degree, enabled him to represent whatever he understood better than any other painter. His animals, particularly lions and horses, are so admirable that it might be said they were never properly represented but by him. . . . The difference of the manner of Rubens from that of any other painter before him, is in nothing more distinguishable than in his coloring. . . . The effect of his pictures may be not improperly compared to clusters of flowers . . . at the same time he has avoided the tawdry effect which one would expect such gay col-ors to produce. . . . To conclude: I will venture to repeat in favor of Rubens what I have before said in regard to the Dutch School—that those who cannot see the extraordinary merit of this great painter either have a narrow conception of the variety of art, or are led away by the affectation of approving nothing but what comes from the Italian School."

Sixty years after Reynolds, the French Romanticist Eugène Delacroix was insistently attracted to Rubens. Unlike Reynolds, who thought Rubens deficient in the way he expressed the emotions, Delacroix wrote with admiration of his sublime mastery of extreme emotion. He, too, was astounded at the technical skill which guided Rubens' "fury of brush" so that the "force, vehemence and splendor" of his conceptions were controlled by "the irresistible swing of a sapient and practiced hand." Delacroix hailed Rubens, by right of imagination and narrative power, as the "Homer of painting."

Renoir, who in mastery of the female nude is one of the few painters to rival Rubens, also studied his technique with admiration—noticing almost ruefully that Rubens achieved with the lightest of touches effects which he himself had tried to achieve by a thick impasto.

Vincent van Gogh was more divided in his opinion. He thought Rubens' religious pictures theatrical, but was impressed by his capacity to express mood by means of color and by the marvelous assurance and speed of his drawing. He was touched by the "pathos and intimacy" in Rubens' portraits of his wives, and excited by his dazzling treatment of fair women. "Just because of Rubens I am looking for a blonde mod-el," he wrote in 1885.

Since the late 1950s the artistic fashion has been moving once again in favor of Rubens, as the appreciation of Baroque art has increased and spread. But Rubens is much more than the greatest Baroque painter of the North. His creative genius is of that comprehensive kind that speaks in different languages to different ages. The work of such masters, whether in literature or music or the visual arts, appeals at many levels and in many ways. Reading the present into the past, each generation instinc-tively finds the elements that have the greatest meaning for it.

Rubens painted to give pleasure. He sought, through the medium of his art, to record the beauty of all created things. A happy and believ-ing man, uniquely endowed by a generous Providence, he seems to call on us to join him in an exuberant psalm of gratitude for the material beauty of the world—"O all ye works of the Lord, bless ye the Lord: praise Him, and magnify Him forever."

The Sunset Decade

The last 10 years of Rubens' life were among his happiest and most satisfying. Save for occasional attacks of gout, which temporarily disabled him, he enjoyed vigorous good health. His second marriage gave him the companionship of a lovely woman, who bore him five children to add to the two surviving from his first family. After a long and busy career as a diplomat, he had obtained permission to retire from that role. Years of successful commissions had made him a wealthy man: his personal collection of paintings included a dozen Pieter Brueghels, 10 Titians and pictures by Raphael, Veronese, Tintoretto, Dürer, Holbein and van Eyck, not to mention nearly 100 of his own valuable works. In addition to his art collection he owned his house and studio in Antwerp and a château at Steen, near a small village some 18 miles south of the city.

During these last years, Rubens' position enabled him to choose his clients, among them King Philip IV of Spain, who pressed on him one last great commission. When he was not working, he rode horseback through the country for hours, renewing his old love of nature. At his easel he drew upon the treasury of his experience, creating gardens of love, peaceful landscapes, peasant frolics. His creative powers reached a new high. In his final works, which recaptured the airy lightness and freedom of some of his earlier oil sketches, he created an art to which future generations would turn in gratitude.

In a mood of happy domesticity, Rubens' wife, Hélène, holds her son Frans while daughter Clara Johanna stands at her knee. This painting, unfinished in some of its background detail, is more than merely a literal portrait of Rubens' beloved family; it is a moving evocation of motherhood as well.

*Hélène Fourment
and Two of Her Children,* c. 1635

A Last Royal Request

In 1636, Philip IV, who subsequently owned more pictures by Rubens than any other collector, commissioned his former diplomat to provide decorations for a 25-room hunting lodge he was building near Madrid. They were to be mythological scenes from Ovid's *Metamorphoses,* an epic poem about the horrible or wonderful things the gods did to those who irritated or pleased them. Despite recurring attacks of gout, during the following year and a half Rubens produced 112 oil sketches. He was to translate only a few into finished paintings; many were completed by assistants and colleagues.

The five shown here are typical of the series; free, loose and powerful, they demonstrate that Rubens' hand had lost none of its strength, his imagination none of its force. Creamy and golden in tone, the oils seem to retain their liquid form, so fluid are Rubens' brushstrokes. This quality, characteristic of his sketching technique throughout his life, is especially evident in his later manner of painting.

Cupid Riding on a Dolphin, c. 1637-1638

The Rape of Hippodameia, c. 1637-1638

The Apotheosis of Hercules, c. 1637-1638

The Fall of Phaeton, c. 1637-1638

The Fall of the Titans, c. 1637-1638

On his rides through the countryside around Steen, Rubens refreshed his acquaintance with the world of Pieter Bruegel—the world of the peasants, at work or at their lusty, and often drunken, pleasures. During his rounds he must have seen many a *kermesse,* or village festival. Like the elder Bruegel, his Flemish forebear, and his contemporary Adriaen Brouwer, who had previously painted such scenes, Rubens understood

peasant life. His exuberant painting shown here is an explosion of energy: a hundred or more men, women and children are gathered outside an inn, drinking, yelling, brawling, dancing, loving—and not forgetting to feed the babies or to pour more liquor down the throat of the man too drunk to fetch his own. The scene is as much the product of the artist's imagination as were earlier mythological works; it could be a Feast of Venus.

La Kermesse, c. 1635-1638

While Rubens was occupied with the great royal commissions of his middle years he painted few landscapes, but in the twilight of his life he returned to nature. In his last decade he is thought to have created some 50 outdoor scenes. Using the free, fluid style that he had evolved, and probably for no other reason than to satisfy himself—17 of the landscapes were among his possessions at his death—Rubens painted the land he had

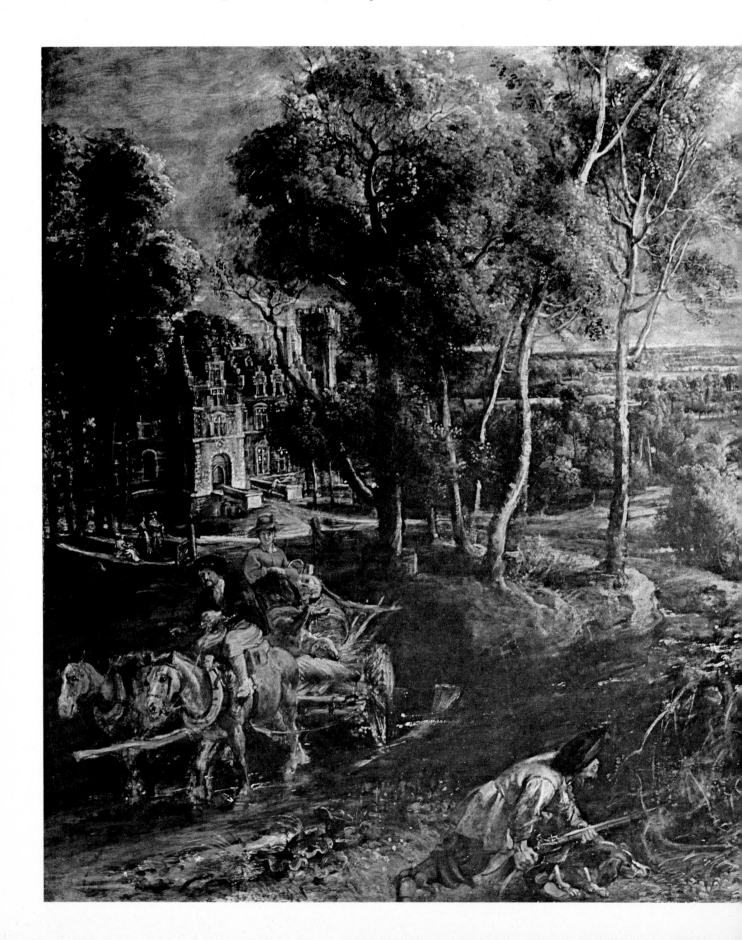

looked at so long and lovingly. Marvels of light and color, these pictures are often more personal, more deeply felt, than many of the grand scenes he had painted before. Here the energy of those earlier works is passionately restated in each sure brushstroke; the color is luminous, outlines are softened, the light seems almost to come from within. In the sunset picture of his home shown here, Rubens' vision of the world is that of a pure painter.

Château de Steen, c. 1635-1637

A few years before his death, Rubens painted the elegant self-portrait below; it reveals the same sensitive intelligence that sparkles from the eyes of his self-portrait as a bridegroom *(page 17)*. Revitalized by a new young family, secure in his profession and his position in society, Rubens continued to paint at his country home *(right)* and in Antwerp until, on May 30, 1640, an attack of gout brought about heart failure and he died.

Self-Portrait, c. 1638-1640

Chronology: Artists of Rubens' Era

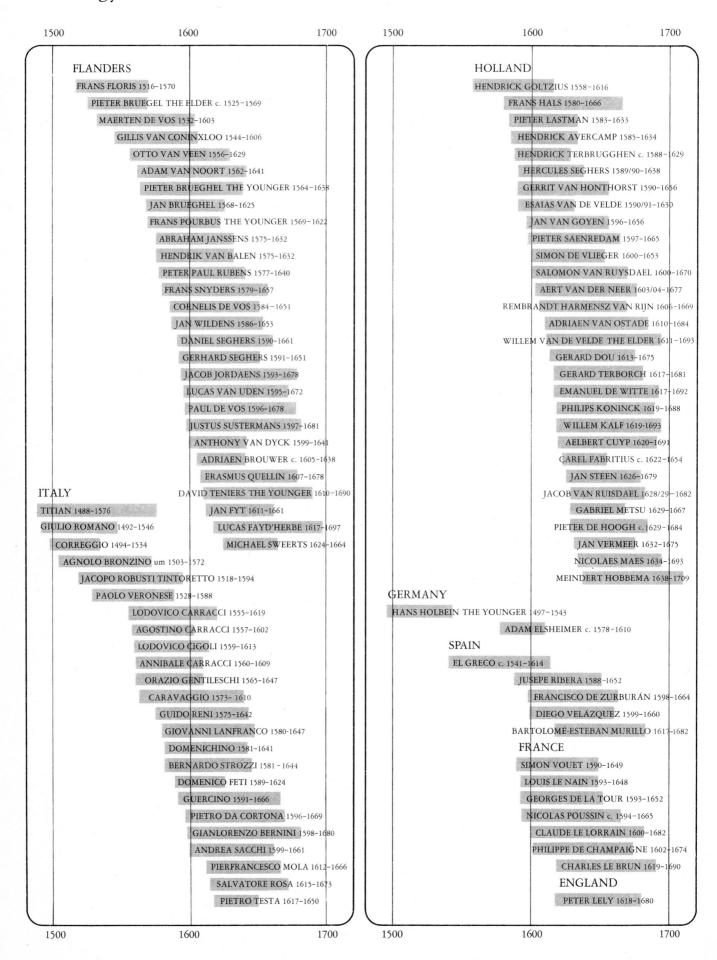

1500   1600   1700   1500   1600   1700

FLANDERS

FRANS FLORIS 1516–1570
PIETER BRUEGEL THE ELDER c. 1525–1569
MAERTEN DE VOS 1532–1603
GILLIS VAN CONINXLOO 1544–1606
OTTO VAN VEEN 1556–1629
ADAM VAN NOORT 1562–1641
PIETER BRUEGHEL THE YOUNGER 1564–1638
JAN BRUEGHEL 1568–1625
FRANS POURBUS THE YOUNGER 1569–1622
ABRAHAM JANSSENS 1575–1632
HENDRIK VAN BALEN 1575–1632
PETER PAUL RUBENS 1577–1640
FRANS SNYDERS 1579–1657
CORNELIS DE VOS 1584–1651
JAN WILDENS 1586–1653
DANIEL SEGHERS 1590–1661
GERHARD SEGHERS 1591–1651
JACOB JORDAENS 1593–1678
LUCAS VAN UDEN 1595–1672
PAUL DE VOS 1596–1678
JUSTUS SUSTERMANS 1597–1681
ANTHONY VAN DYCK 1599–1641
ADRIAEN BROUWER c. 1605–1638
ERASMUS QUELLIN 1607–1678
DAVID TENIERS THE YOUNGER 1610–1690

ITALY

TITIAN 1488–1576
GIULIO ROMANO 1492–1546
CORREGGIO 1494–1534
AGNOLO BRONZINO um 1503–1572
JACOPO ROBUSTI TINTORETTO 1518–1594
PAOLO VERONESE 1528–1588
LODOVICO CARRACCI 1555–1619
AGOSTINO CARRACCI 1557–1602
LODOVICO CIGOLI 1559–1613
ANNIBALE CARRACCI 1560–1609
ORAZIO GENTILESCHI 1565–1647
CARAVAGGIO 1573–1610
GUIDO RENI 1575–1642
GIOVANNI LANFRANCO 1580–1647
DOMENICHINO 1581–1641
BERNARDO STROZZI 1581–1644
DOMENICO FETI 1589–1624
GUERCINO 1591–1666
PIETRO DA CORTONA 1596–1669
GIANLORENZO BERNINI 1598–1680
ANDREA SACCHI 1599–1661
PIERFRANCESCO MOLA 1612–1666
SALVATORE ROSA 1615–1673
PIETRO TESTA 1617–1650

JAN FYT 1611–1661
LUCAS FAYD'HERBE 1617–1697
MICHAEL SWEERTS 1624–1664

HOLLAND

HENDRICK GOLTZIUS 1558–1616
FRANS HALS 1580–1666
PIETER LASTMAN 1583–1633
HENDRICK AVERCAMP 1585–1634
HENDRICK TERBRUGGHEN c. 1588–1629
HERCULES SEGHERS 1589/90–1638
GERRIT VAN HONTHORST 1590–1656
ESAIAS VAN DE VELDE 1590/91–1630
JAN VAN GOYEN 1596–1656
PIETER SAENREDAM 1597–1665
SIMON DE VLIEGER 1600–1653
SALOMON VAN RUYSDAEL 1600–1670
AERT VAN DER NEER 1603/04–1677
REMBRANDT HARMENSZ VAN RIJN 1606–1669
ADRIAEN VAN OSTADE 1610–1684
WILLEM VAN DE VELDE THE ELDER 1611–1693
GERARD DOU 1613–1675
GERARD TERBORCH 1617–1681
EMANUEL DE WITTE 1617–1692
PHILIPS KONINCK 1619–1688
WILLEM KALF 1619–1693
AELBERT CUYP 1620–1691
CAREL FABRITIUS c. 1622–1654
JAN STEEN 1626–1679
JACOB VAN RUISDAEL 1628/29–1682
GABRIEL METSU 1629–1667
PIETER DE HOOGH c. 1629–1684
JAN VERMEER 1632–1675
NICOLAES MAES 1634–1693
MEINDERT HOBBEMA 1638–1709

GERMANY

HANS HOLBEIN THE YOUNGER 1497–1543
ADAM ELSHEIMER c. 1578–1610

SPAIN

EL GRECO c. 1541–1614
JUSEPE RIBERA 1588–1652
FRANCISCO DE ZURBURÁN 1598–1664
DIEGO VELÁZQUEZ 1599–1660
BARTOLOMÉ-ESTEBAN MURILLO 1617–1682

FRANCE

SIMON VOUET 1590–1649
LOUIS LE NAIN 1593–1648
GEORGES DE LA TOUR 1593–1652
NICOLAS POUSSIN c. 1594–1665
CLAUDE LE LORRAIN 1600–1682
PHILIPPE DE CHAMPAIGNE 1602–1674
CHARLES LE BRUN 1619–1690

ENGLAND

PETER LELY 1618–1680

1500   1600   1700   1500   1600   1700

Rubens' predecessors and contemporaries are grouped here in chronological order according to country. The bands correspond to the life-spans of the artists.

Bibliography   *Paperback

RUBENS—LIFE AND WORK

Burchard, Ludwig, and R. A. d'Hulst, *Rubens' Drawings*, 2 vols. Arcade Press, Brussels, 1958. A selection of drawings, illustrated and described.

Burckhardt, Jacob, *Recollections of Rubens*. Phaidon Press, Ltd., London, 1950. An essay on the artist's personality by a late-19th Century historian.

Cammaerts, Emile, *Rubens: Painter and Diplomat*. Faber and Faber, Ltd., London, 1932. A concise, general biography.

Encyclopedia of World Art, Vol. XII. McGraw-Hill, 1966. Includes a compact biography and bibliography of Rubens by Michael Jaffé.

Goris, Jan-Albert, and Julius S. Held, *Rubens in America*. Pantheon Books, Inc., 1947. An illustrated catalogue of the paintings and drawings known to be in American collections in 1947.

Held, Julius S., *Rubens, Selected Drawings*, 2 vols. Phaidon Press, Ltd., London, 1959. A well-illustrated analysis of drawings and oil sketches.

L'Art en Belgique, Vol. VI: *Rubens et la Peinture Baroque*. Foundation Cultura, Brussels. A portfolio of excellent color reproductions of works by Rubens and other Flemish painters.

Lind, L. R. (translator), "The Latin Life of Peter Paul Rubens by his Nephew Philip." *Art Quarterly*, Vol. IX, 1946, pp. 37-44. An English translation of a near-contemporary's interesting biographical sketch.

MacLaren, N., *Peter Paul Rubens, The Château de Steen*. Gallery Books, London, 1946. An appreciation of the artist's late landscape style.

Magurn, Ruth Saunders (translator and editor), *The Letters of Peter Paul Rubens*. Harvard University Press, 1955. All of Rubens' known letters, annotated.

Michel, Emile, *Rubens: His Life, His Work and His Time*, 2 vols. Charles Scribner's Sons, 1899. A good, lengthy survey.

Myers, Mary L., "Rubens and the Woodcuts of Christoffel Jegher." *The Metropolitan Museum of Art Bulletin*, Summer, 1956, pp. 7-23.

Puyvelde, Leo van, *The Sketches of Rubens*. Translated by Eveline Winkworth. Routledge and Kegan Paul, Ltd., London, 1947. An interpretive study.

Rooses, Max, *Rubens*, 2 vols. Translated by Harold Child. Duckworth and Co., 1904. A somewhat dated but valuable biography.

Sainsbury, W. Noel (editor), *Original Unpublished Papers Illustrative of the Life of Sir Peter Paul Rubens*. Bradbury & Evans, London, 1859. A collection of significant letters and other documents by Rubens' contemporaries.

ART-HISTORICAL BACKGROUND

Dupont, Jacques, and François Mathey, *The Seventeenth Century*. Translated by S.J.C. Harrison. Albert Skira, Geneva. A pictorial survey of artistic developments from Caravaggio to Vermeer.

Fromentin, Eugène, *The Old Masters of Belgium and Holland*.* Schocken Books, 1963. A personal, critical commentary by the 19th Century artist-author.

Gerson, H., and E. H. Ter Kuile, *Art and Architecture in Belgium: 1600-1800*. Penguin Books, 1960. A useful illustrated study with a good bibliography.

Hauser, Arnold, *The Social History of Art*, Vol. 2.* Vintage Books, 1960. A comprehensive analysis.

Jaffé, Michael, *Van Dyck's Antwerp Sketchbook*. McDonald, London, 1966. A complete edition of the sketchbook kept by van Dyck as a very young man working closely with Rubens.

Lassaigne, Jacques, and Robert L. Delevoy, *Flemish Painting*. Albert Skira, Geneva, 1958. A survey of art from Hieronymus Bosch to Rubens, with color illustrations.

Wittkower, Rudolf, *Art and Architecture in Italy: 1600-1750*. Penguin Books, 1958. An important general study covering some of Rubens' Italian contemporaries.

CULTURAL AND HISTORICAL BACKGROUND

Friedrich, Carl J., *The Age of the Baroque*.* Harper Torchbooks, 1952. A history of European politics, economics and culture from 1610-1660.

Geyl, Pieter, *The Netherlands in the Seventeenth Century*. Barnes and Noble, Inc., 1961. A reliable and complete survey.

Ogg, David, *Europe in the Seventeenth Century*. Adam and Charles Black, London, 1948. A study of the politics and personalities of the period.

Wedgwood, C. V., *The Thirty Years War*.* Doubleday and Co., Inc., 1961. A thorough history of the European war that lasted from 1618 to 1648.

Acknowledgments

The editors of this book wish to thank the following people and institutions: Fedja Anzelewski, Kupferstichkabinet, Staatliche Museum of Berlin; Erwin Maria Auer, Director, Kunsthistorisches Museum, Vienna; Frans Baudouin, Conservateur, Kunsthistorisches Museum, Antwerp; Luisa Becherucci, Soprintendenza alle Gallerie, Florence; Armand Bérard, French Embassy, Rome; Boymans van Beuningen Museum, Rotterdam; British Museum, Prints and Drawings Room, London; Liselotte Camp, Alte Pinakothek, Munich; Walter Koschatzky, Graphische Sammlung Albertina, Vienna; Georg J. Kugler, Kunsthistorisches Museum, Vienna; Frits Lugt, Président de l'Institut Néerlandais, Paris; Frans Maes, Director, Joseph Kadijk, Deputy Director, Gerda Heinman, Librarian, and staff, Belgian Information Service, New York; Paul Maison, Château de Steen, Elewyt, Belgium; Ministry of Public Building and Works, London; Museum Plantin-Moretus, Antwerp; René Pendelaers, Assistant, Kunsthistorisches Museum, Antwerp; Ugo Procacci, Soprintendente alle Gallerie, Florence; Paul Provost, Musée Bonnat, Bayonne; Hans-Heinrich Richter, Deutsche Fotothek, Dresden; Rubens House, Antwerp; Pierre Schneider; Stedelijk Museum, Amsterdam; Carlos van Hasselt, Conservateur, Institut Néerlandais, Paris; Léon Voet, Conservateur, Museum Plantin-Moretus, Antwerp.

Picture Credits

The sources for the illustrations in this book appear below. Credits for pictures from left to right are separated by semicolons, from top to bottom by dashes.

MUSEO DEL PRADO, MADRID

Rubens' drawings for woodcuts reproduced on the end papers of this book are based on the painting above, *The Garden of Love*. An exuberant scene painted late in his career, it reflects Rubens' happiness during his last 10 years of life with a pretty wife and a new family.

Index

Index (continued)

Printed in Spain by Printer industria gráfica sa   Provenza, 388   Barcelona-25   Depósito legal B. 12442-1978